Flying Solo

Robert Gerrish has been flying solo since 1990 with businesses in London and Sydney. He coaches soloists, delivers talks and workshops, presents on radio and writes regular columns for News Limited and *My Business* magazine. A recent measure of success was when his 4-year-old son didn't realise he actually did any work. His wife, Jane, however, is pleased that he does.

Sam Leader is a professional writer and, of course, a soloist. Her experience of transitioning from worker bee to queen of her own hive makes her well placed to advise others looking to make the jump. She lives in Sydney's northern beaches with her partner, John-Paul.

Flying Solo

How to go it alone in business

Robert Gerrish and Sam Leader

ALLEN&UNWIN

First published in 2005

Allen & Unwin
85 Alexander Street
Crows Nest NSW 2065
Australia
Phone: (61 2) 8425 0100
Fax: (61 2) 9906 2218
Email: info@allenandunwin.com
Web: www.allenandunwin.com

National Library of Australia
Cataloguing-in-Publication entry:

Gerrish, Robert
    Flying Solo : how to go it alone in business

    Bibliography.
    ISBN 1 74114 424 8.

    1. Self-employed. 2. Small business - Management
    3. Success in business. I. Leader, Sam. II. Title.

658.041

Typeset in 10.5/13.5pt Sabon by Midland Typesetters
Maryborough, Victoria
Printed by McPherson's Printing Group, Victoria

10 9 8 7 6 5 4 3 2 1

Flying Solo is dedicated to the world's actual and aspiring soloists.

CONTENTS

Introduction: Welcome to the soloists' century   1

Thinking solo   15

1 The soloists' paradigm   17
2 Adopting the attitude of success   33
3 The power of vision   47

Acting solo   65

4 Developing your game plan   67
5 Spreading the word   89
6 Eight essentials for a healthy solo business   109

Staying solo   141

7 Keeping on track   143
8 The soloist's manifesto   163

Bibliography   167

INTRODUCTION
WELCOME TO THE SOLOISTS' CENTURY

An invasion of armies can be resisted, but not an idea whose time has come.

Victor Hugo

In the past, individuals who have chosen to go it alone in business have had to jostle for space in the professional arena alongside more dominant, traditional workstyles. Corporatism in particular, exemplified by the 9 to 5 office job, characterised the way we worked throughout the twentieth century. But at the dawn of the 2000s it appears we are on the cusp of something quite remarkable, with record numbers of individuals stampeding to soloism.

Ladies and gentleman, welcome to the soloists' century.

Yes, corporatism's poor relation has finally emerged from the shadows and is enjoying a prestige of its own. It has grown to the extent that today, of all businesses in operation in the US and UK, an incredible two-thirds are solo ventures.

And the number keeps on growing.

In Australia in 1997, there were fewer than 300 000 soloists. By 2003 that number had rocketed to over 800 000 (nearly 70 per cent of the nation's small businesses). Throughout the world, these figures continue to climb as people find the fulfilment they seek through being the architects of their own careers. If you want to join them, this book will help.

The great news is soloism is more democratic and accessible than ever before as we are presented with opportunities that simply didn't exist a decade or so ago. Back then, most of us saw soloism as the preserve of a small band of audacious entrepreneurs. In contrast, today we are encouraged by the sight of people like us starting their own enterprises. 'If others can do it,' we ask, 'why can't I?'

The easy answer? You can!

For proof of how many people are seizing the opportunity to jump on this new wave, put your ear to the wall and you'll hear the buzz of spare rooms and garages being transformed into home offices. Look out of the window and you'll see an army of individuals turning their backs on soulless careers, opting instead to spread their wings and fly solo. If you're ready to join them, there's never been a better time to do so. The force really is with you.

Of course, taking the plunge is one thing; getting it right is quite another. If you're a soloist who is struggling to cope, *Flying Solo* will act as the aphrodisiac you need to fall back in love with your business. We will help those who have lost their way and would-be soloists alike by showing you how to build a soloist venture you will want to cherish. Prepare to be probed, as we'll be asking lots of questions to get you on course. Questions like: What do you want to get out of soloism? What do you have to offer? What is it that drives you? Discover the answers in upcoming chapters and before you know it you'll be joining the modern business revolution.

SOME GREAT THINGS ABOUT SOLOISM

You have to love your work because few things are as crucial to your overall happiness as how you feel about what you do. Soloism provides the ideal solution for those seeking to balance their desire for professional satisfaction with their personal needs. Get it right, and soloism can:

- transform your working life from one where you feel obligated to one where you feel liberated;
- make it possible for you to design and create your dream job;
- enable you to get personal and professional satisfaction from your work;
- enable you to keep your own hours and balance your work and lifestyle commitments;
- give you the freedom to fully express yourself through your work;
- make you jump out of bed from Monday to Friday, instead of hitting the snooze button and hiding under the covers.

WHY *FLYING SOLO* IS DIFFERENT

In spite of soloism's seemingly unstoppable growth, it remains poorly charted territory. Until *Flying Solo*, countless people have been forced to navigate the stormy skies of soloism without a decent map. This lack of relevant information has caused plenty of individuals to suffer a mid-air collision, with many more would-be soloists dismissing the idea of taking off altogether.

The problem is, in part, that when those with the soloist itch seek guidance from the business section of any bookshop, they'll find row upon row of textbook-style guides on 'how to run a small business' which focus on the matter-of-fact, practical parts of soloism such as the financial and legal elements.

Knowing the practicalities of running your own business is important but, we believe, is really just the half of it. You may be able to do your accounting in your sleep, but if your heart's not in your business, you'll find it hard to get going, let alone keep going. *Flying Solo* emphasises what's required of you both practically and psychologically. We'll ensure your solo business doesn't suffer, as so many do, because of a misaligned head and heart. This inside-out rather than outside-in approach will help make sure your stab at soloism doesn't end up one of the sorry statistics of small business failures.

The dizzying array of books that imply your solo business is all but worthless unless it can be turned into a worldwide empire makes soloists even more discouraged. This 'bigger, better, faster' assumption is *so* last century and sorely misses the point, at least according to most of the soloists we talk to. For them, soloism is about the connection, not the career. They seek to nurture a business that is an expression of themselves and their values. They would rather keep things manageable and meaningful than sweat about growth and profits, thank you very much. The idea that a soloist business should be run like a micro version of a multinational is not only outmoded, but is actually at the root of many a soloist's misery.

This book espouses the revolutionary philosophy that a solo business should be run like . . . a solo business!

Flying Solo gives the advice you need to realise your dreams of autonomy and answers questions like:

- What's involved in being my own boss?
- How can I turn my dreams into concrete goals?
- What foundations are needed for my solo business?
- How do I get my idea out into the world?
- How do I keep my business on track?

If you're tempted by the rewards but don't know enough about what's involved, or if you harbour doubts as to whether you've got what it takes, you're sure to find *Flying Solo* inspiring. It may also happen that as you progress through the book you realise you're not suited to soloism. If that's the case, at least we'll have helped you make an informed choice.

WHAT IS A SOLOIST?

The dictionary's current definition of soloist is a little too narrow for our purposes. It appears as follows:

> **soloist** *n.* a performer of a solo, esp. in music

Our definition of a soloist is someone who generates their own income by working for themselves. With the trend becoming more prevalent, it's only a matter of time before this definition appears in the dictionary, so you can expect future editions to look like this:

soloist *n*. 1. an individual who runs their own enterprise. 2. a performer of a solo, esp. in music

If our prophecy is correct, this will appear above it:

soloism *n*. a system of independent enterprises run by individuals

Soloists have the following in common:

- They are self-employed.
- They mostly work alone, although occasionally in a partnership or small team.
- Their income is reliant on their capacity to make it.
- Their past experiences contribute in some way to their current direction.

Broadly speaking, there are two categories of soloist: the independent professional and the micro or small business owner.

Independent professionals are soloists who sell their expertise for a fee. They may also choose to be known as consultants, contractors, freelancers, free agents or independents. This group includes, although is not limited to, the following:

accountants
architects
artists
bookkeepers
business coaches
computer technicians
event organisers
financial planners
graphic designers
homoeopaths
HR consultants
independent real estate
  agents
insurance consultants
interior designers
IT consultants

lawyers

life coaches

management consultants

massage therapists

musicians

naturopaths

PR consultants

personal trainers

photographers

product designers

professional speakers

publicists

quantity surveyors

recruitment consultants

sponsorship executives

strategists

systems analysts

therapists

virtual assistants

web designers

web developers

writers

Micro/small business owners are soloists who are involved at a decision-making level within any micro, small or family business. Examples of this group include franchise holders, retail outlet owners, restaurant and café owners, and trades-people such as carpenters, construction workers, electricians and plumbers.

In the past, these lines of work would have been divided into 'white' and 'blue' collar professions, but the spirit of soloism dictates these oppressive titles be thrown out the window. There's no room for prejudice in Soloville, where the playing fields are perfectly level. Soloville is a place where you define your job, not vice versa. Its national anthem would be the classic 'It ain't what you do, it's the way that you do it' (preferably sung by Ella Fitzgerald, not Bananarama). We'll be elaborating on this delectable theme throughout the book.

In the meantime here's a description of the nation of Soloville's patriots.

Born soloists are those with innate talents, for example, athletes, artists, writers and performers such as actors, singers and musicians. Only a handful of born soloists recognise their abilities at an early age. More usually, they fall into one of the following categories.

Soloists by design are those who deliberately pursue a career as an independent. A broad range inhabits this category, including fresh-faced school leavers and graduates who have never worked for anyone else. These youngsters are giving what their parents would consider a conventional career path a very wide berth. Damian Barr, the 26-year-old author of *Get It Together: Surviving Your Quarterlife Crisis*, observes, 'Increasingly my generation is finding new work styles—we're freelancing . . . running more than one career simultaneously—anything to avoid the nine-to-five trap.'

At the other end of the soloist by design spectrum are those with a history of traditional employment going back decades. Many of these individuals are what we dub 'corporate escapees' who have escaped their jobs when the ladder they thought they wanted to be at the top of turns out to have been leaning against the wrong wall. Often they not only give up their job, but also the high-speed, high-consumption way of life that typically goes with it, opting instead for a lower key, more self-reliant lifestyle. Some experience a shift in values so radical that they choose to overhaul their entire lives. Often called 'sea changers', these individuals could, for example, be managing a European bank one month and running a macadamia nut plantation in New Zealand the next.

Accidental soloists perceive the decision to go solo has been made for them. They haven't sought soloism out; rather, it has found them. When asked to explain how they got to where they are, they answer, 'I sort of fell into it.'

Fate has played a large part in proceedings for the accidental soloist. Something as simple as a friend's off-the-
cuff remark—'I loved that jewellery you made me for my
birthday. Have you ever thought about making stuff
professionally?'—may precipitate their decision to work
alone.

Circumstantial soloists, too, experience changes in their
lives that enable them to accommodate the option of
working for themselves. A large number in this category
are working parents, most commonly mothers, who seek
the income and challenge of a career but are reluctant to
leave their children at home. For them, as for so many,
soloism offers the best of both worlds. Those who experience retrenchment also face a dramatic change in their
working life and in some cases soloism turns out to be the
silver lining to the cloud of losing their job. It was a
catalyst for better things for Paul, a construction project
manager whose severance payment helped to fund his
soloist venture:

> Losing my job turned out to be the best thing that happened
> to me. I hadn't realised how reliant I had been on my
> employer to look after my professional development. Being
> forced to take control of my working life has been tough in
> some ways, but it has ultimately been so rewarding. I've never
> been more fulfilled.

Such soloists may not have considered soloism as an option
or may have dismissed it as a pipedream until events occurred to make them think otherwise. The cards may have
fallen the right way for them, but waiting for circumstances
to conspire in your favour is not recommended. The chances

of you realising your ambitions are far greater if you face up to the challenge of engineering your solo situation for yourself. This book will help you rise to that challenge.

WHY GO FROM SALARIED TO SOLO?

Since the start of the century, the 'salaried to solo' movement has been gaining more momentum than a runaway train. In Australia, for instance, in 2003 businesses run by one person rose to a whopping 69 per cent of total small businesses, and in the same year in Britain over 300 000 workers joined the ranks of the self-employed.

Corporate collapses and mass redundancies go some way to explaining the exodus. These factors, a reality of modern business life, have contributed to the demise of the 'job for life' concept, making soloism seem a less risky option. In this environment people are more inclined to think, 'If I can't count on the security of a salary, why not give working alone a go?' Of those who are in relatively secure employment, many resent the sacrifices they have to make to meet the demands of their job. Free time is the most obvious casualty, with the average Australian's working week increasing in length from 42 to 45 hours between 1982 and the mid-1990s. At the same time, their lunch 'hours' have shrunk to an average of 27 minutes. Workers on the other side of the world are feeling the pressure, too, with 4.8 million UK employees working unpaid overtime in 2004. Both of these trends are reflected throughout the working world.

The pervasiveness of the long hours work culture is observed by Carl Honoré in his bestselling book *In Praise of Slow*: 'Work devours the bulk of our waking hours,' he says.

'Everything else in life—family and friends, sex and sleep, hobbies and holidays—is forced to bend around the almighty work schedule.' According to Neil Crofts, author of *Authentic: How to Make a Living by Being Yourself*, another source of dissatisfaction for people is that they struggle to find purpose in traditional jobs: 'Enough of us recognise our need to understand and realise our own potential and it becomes clear that helping big corporations to become bigger and exploit better fails to deliver that for us.'

When we asked those who had gone from salaried to solo their reasons for doing so, their answers tended to validate the theories of both Croft and Honoré, with the need to regain control over their working lives featuring highly. The desire to pursue dreams of working for themselves proved a major motivator for many, while others saw soloism as a way to break free from stressful, unsatisfying jobs. So it was for financial adviser Tom, who worked for a blue-chip accounting firm where the hours took him to breaking point:

> I was working an average of 60 hours every week and once went from Monday to Friday without seeing my 2-year-old daughter awake. There was always so much to be done at work, I could never get away on time. The next week, exhausted after another long day, I broke down in front of my wife and said, 'There has to be more to life than this.' Until then, I had just assumed my job would improve my family's quality of life. Talking to my wife, I realised the sacrifices I had to make for my job actually made the rest of my life, *our lives*, a whole heap worse. That's when I made the decision to quit.

Tom describes a working environment that is, like thousands of others, ruled by what Carl Honoré, dubs 'a tyranny of speed'. He believes our world's current obsession with getting more done in less time has eliminated our freedom to choose whether to take our time over tasks. As a soloist, you set your own pace, thus seizing back the critical element of choice. Furthermore, we find the happiest soloists succeed not because they compete with the endurance of an iron man, or are über-productive, but because they have the knack for putting work in its proper place alongside the rest of their lives.

While people rarely regret their decision to go solo, it doesn't mean their transitions aren't problematic. Unless you are exceptionally focused and driven, you can expect to feel muddled about the road ahead as you plan your transit from one mode to another. It is hard to act in a job day in and day out—and if you don't feel like yourself at work it really is acting—and simultaneously give consideration to what would be a suitable alternative. The authors of *Careers Un-ltd,* Carmel McConnell and Jonathan Robinson, give the rather wonderful analogy of the 'hammerhead shark' where one eye is on your actual job while the other seeks ways out of it. The process can be complex, but facing up to the issues is the first step towards excavating the real you.

To get the most out of reading *Flying Solo*, allow yourself time and give yourself permission to think through any questions the book raises within you. Let your thoughts brew and when they're ready to percolate, write them on a notepad, jot them down on your PDA or record them on your iPod. This will not only give clarity to your thoughts, but also free up room in your mind for your ideas to keep flowing. Conversation with trusted allies will also help you see your way on the road ahead.

Lives that are imbued with purpose and lived fully don't happen by accident. To make it happen for you, ensure you engage and participate in the process. That's why you shouldn't consider time spent soul-searching as indulgent or wasteful—instead see it as an integral part of the psychological preparation that is at the heart of every successful solo venture.

Let's get your journey underway by providing an insight into the mental space successful soloists occupy. Ready to start thinking solo?

Thought so.

THINKING
SOLO

MASTER HOW SUCCESSFUL SOLOISTS
SEE THE WORLD AND YOU'LL GET TO
SHARE THE VIEW

CHAPTER 1

THE SOLOISTS' PARADIGM

Problems we face cannot be solved at the same level of awareness that created them.

Albert Einstein

Every day, each of us carries a head full of thoughts governing how we act and operate. Where the positive ones will support our goals and dreams, the negative ones can be a major contributor to our demise. Like professional athletes who spend months psychologically preparing for competition, you need to respect the relationship between beliefs and outcomes and be prepared to channel your thoughts in the right direction.

Be clear on this: your outlook will not merely influence your solo journey, but direct it. So to ensure you have a healthy outlook, this chapter will steer you away from attitudes that put a rod on your back and towards those that put a spring in your step.

For example, each of us is likely to be influenced by the opinions of others. You may be lucky and be surrounded by an army of advocates, but realistically you can expect to encounter some negativity when you voice your plans for soloism. Unfortunately, every cynical eyebrow and well-meaning warning can act like a guy rope on your hot-air balloon—plus you need to cope with your own insecurities. Every hackle raised by your 'inner heckler' could create a further mental barrier to your goals. When you are committed to your plan of flying solo, you owe it to yourself to rise above all this. Soloist David sums it up:

> The best thing I ever did . . . was to consciously and persistently beat out all the negative reasons why the business would not work. If anyone offered a pessimistic view of why I should not fly solo I would combat that with several reasons why I should.

Get ready to sharpen your knife and cut free from the ropes holding you back.

OLD ASSUMPTIONS, NEW REALITIES

Once you understand what is driving your detractors, you can put their perceptions into perspective. Objections to soloism are often voiced by those with what we call an 'old assumptions' view: basically a rigid set of expectations of the way we ought to work. According to old assumers, soloist ventures are no substitute for a proper job. This notoriously conservative lot favour security and prescribed behaviour, which completely contrasts with soloists, who champion innovation and free thinking.

Old assumers' negativity is fuelled by misconceptions and prejudices relating to soloism. Examples of their objections, which we'll rebut in detail later, include:

- You'll only be productive if you work long hours.
- Most small businesses end quickly in financial ruin.
- It is important to wear a suit to work.
- You can't expect to enjoy your job.
- Material wealth is the most accurate measure of success.
- Real work only gets done in real offices.
- Soloists miss out on the social element of work.
- It is better to work hard now so you can enjoy life later.

Old assumptions are prevalent in our society's traditional-ist work culture, and may well have wormed their way into your psyche. If so, it's time to exorcise them. The fact is soloists need old assumptions like a fish needs a bicycle. Through this perilously narrow perspective it would be easy to dismiss soloism as too avant-garde and risky. In addition, an overly cautious outlook limits your exposure to ideas and opportunities and panders to any less ambi-tious expectations you may have of yourself.

Instead you need to think about soloism in a consid-ered, not a conditioned way. So why not subscribe to a philosophy that champions the choices you make as an independent? We've come up with an alternative, more productive paradigm for you, called the 'new reality'. This revolutionary take on the concept of work challenges old assumptions about business basics by embracing the prag-matism and independence soloists need like oxygen.

Of course, how you view the world is totally up to you. If the soloist in you is to flourish, though, only one school of thought gives you wings, while the other effectively clips them. You'll see what we mean when you look at the words/phrases favoured by each philosophy:

Old assumption	New reality
Organisation	Individual
Comfort zone	Unknown
Work to make a living	Work to have a life
Pursue a job for life	Pursue the spice of life
Measure success objectively	Measure success holistically
Reality is objective	Reality is subjective
'I ought, I must'	'I think, I believe'
Happiness is a bonus	Happiness is a right
Resist change	Respond to change
Competition	Co-opetition (see next chapter)
Wait for things to happen	Make things happen
By the book	On the fly
Replicate	Innovate
Cautious	Intrepid
Dogmatic	Pragmatic
Focus on the past	Focus on the present
Work first, play later	Work and play together
Risk-averse	Accepting of risk

Surprisingly, becoming a soloist is as much about unlearning old behaviours as it is about learning new ones. At the centre of your journey is the need to reacquaint yourself with your true motivations while extricating yourself from damaging elements of the herd mentality. Neil Crofts further justifies this when he says:

> Most of us are brought up to believe others have a more real interpretation of the world than we do. This results in our learning not to trust, or very often even listen to, our instincts. Being honest with ourselves seems hard to start

with, we have years of conditioning to break, but once we make the leap it is harder still not to be.

To help you respond to the challenge of contending with your own, and others', suspicious minds, we've elaborated on some common old assumptions and countered them with arguments based on the soloists' new reality. Our pro-solo arguments challenge old assumptions about work in general and reject claims made about the specifics of soloism. Get ready to arm yourself with this arsenal of intelligent arguments, and you will be disarming the doubters in no time!

Assumption 1: You'll only be productive if you work long hours

This old assumption states time spent at work is more important than the quality of the work done. While the lady who lunches 'aldesko' and works endless overtime is considered committed, Mr 9-to-5 who uses non-work time to exercise is deemed a slacker. Never mind she takes more sick leave and feels permanently exhausted while he's firing on all cylinders.

The widespread culture of 'presenteeism' has taken its toll on job satisfaction. An international survey undertaken by UK economists has found that 70 per cent of people in twenty-seven countries wanted a better work/life balance.

The good news is, as a soloist, you're not obliged to subscribe to the conventional 'wisdom' that you work like a dog all week and recover on the weekend. You don't need permission to take a break from anyone other than yourself, but if you're used to toiling under the 'longer hours = better worker' model, you could feel guilty about taking time out. In his book *Right & Wrong*, sociologist Hugh Mackay observes, 'many people . . . have decided busyness is the great modern virtue . . . as though a slackened pace may be a sign of weakness or failure'. With this attitude prevailing in a world where the tyranny of speed rules, it's scarcely surprising that you might feel uneasy subscribing to this new reality. While it may initially be hard for you to take a breather at times you believe you should be working, just give it a try and it'll become apparent that not only does the sky not fall down because of your absence, it actually starts to look a whole lot bluer.

Commit to taking a break and you will benefit from:

- clearer thinking, improved concentration and better responsiveness;
- a better relationship with your business, because time off allows you to feel more engaged with—and less harried by—your work;
- a sense of control over your time and business, resulting in better time/business management;
- a more harmonious relationship with your well-being as you develop the knack for listening and responding to your body's requests, which often go ignored when you're powering through—for example, 'I'm so hungry but haven't got time to eat';
- enhanced self-respect and confidence;
- full assimilation of the principles of work/life balance.

Abraham Lincoln famously said, 'If I had six hours to cut down a tree, I'd spend the first four hours sharpening the axe.' During the work day, be sure to devote time to activities which replenish your energies or sharpen your axe.

Assumption 2: Most small businesses end quickly in financial ruin

Haunting statistics are, arguably, the biggest deterrent for would-be soloists, but we believe the definition of 'failure' is unfairly broad. For example, a good number of soloists will at some stage choose to adjust their direction, even sell or merge their enterprise. They do so to realise the value, financial or otherwise, of the contribution they have made to their business, maybe because they have outgrown their original venture or have chosen to explore different opportunities. Then there are small percentages of soloists whose businesses cease simply because they have run their natural course; it's time to move in a different direction, live in another country, perhaps!

Somehow, though, it seems when *any* soloist goes through the natural process of change, whatever the outcome, they are lumped together into the category of 'failure'. When a non-soloist changes his job, is it because he failed in the last one? No, it is because he has evolved in a different direction. Soloists deserve the same level of flexibility.

The best soloist businesses react in tandem with their owner, but those that leave the soloist no room to manoeuvre when they want to change or move on are, unfortunately, very common. You can avoid making these errors by following the advice in the 'Acting Solo' section of the book, where we highlight best practices for soloists.

Assumption 3: It is important to wear a suit to work

Stephanie, an accountant, tells the story of how she successfully challenged this old assumption:

> I always hated wearing a suit to work. But after I left my job to fly solo, the old assumer in me dictated I should dress formally to meet my clients. After a while, it was getting to a point where I felt as if I couldn't face myself. I seriously thought it through, then bit the bullet and told clients I planned to dress down for meetings. One in particular disapproved and soon after we parted company. But I never felt we were on the same wavelength so was philosophical about losing his business. Overwhelmingly, though, my clients told me they respected my honesty. I've been able to turn it into a feature of my offering and now seem to attract clients who prefer not to dress formally to meetings.
>
> It's really taught me the merits of being honest in my business. I know my clients are working with me, not some masked identity I assume between 9 and 5 on Mondays to Fridays.

In the land of new realities, it is possible to pit your individual integrity against external expectations with great results. If you feel you're wearing the wrong outfit every day, chances are you're in the wrong job. Don't ignore this, or any other indicators that signal the need for change.

Assumption 4: You can't expect to enjoy your job

Or alternatively, 'work is just something you have to do to survive'. Most of us spend more of our time working than we do with friends and family. When such a massive part of your life is devoted to work, how can you possibly not owe it to yourself to find a vocation that is rewarding? The new reality states that if you're not passionate about what you're doing, do something else. Constantly ignore your dissatisfaction or persist in following carrots that secretly don't interest you and your self-respect will implode during a spectacular midlife—or quarterlife—crisis. Consider this quote from Michaelangelo: 'The greatest danger for most of us is not that our aim is too high and we miss it, but that it is too low and we hit it.' Do whatever it takes to make your work work.

Assumption 5: Material wealth is the most accurate measure of success

Judging by the number of people whose primary ambition is to secure a highly paid job, this old assumption has succeeded in seeping its way into conventional wisdom. What is apparent, though, is that the dogged pursuit of money all too often comes at the expense of emotional energy. This is demonstrated by the 'golden handcuffs' syndrome, where well-paid individuals feel bound to a high-consumption lifestyle they find draining and dissatisfying, but hard to escape from. Those who struggle to separate the meaning of their work from its trappings are in danger of experiencing the horrible sensation of feeling like strangers in their own skin.

Today's new reality is that people are realising economic achievement may be a measure of success, but it's not the only measure. In some cases, people question whether it is any sort of yardstick at all. A 2003 Newspoll survey indicates as many as 40 per cent of Australians have sought ways of making changes in their professional circumstances in a bid to simplify their lives. Amongst those are so-called high achievers who have traded lucrative jobs to become soloists. Those who get the most from the trade-in know that what they lose in income they gain in terms of happier relationships, improved health and a better sense of control over their lives. They choose to focus on what they have, rather than on what they do not have.

This new reality turns the 'time is money' concept on its head and is perhaps the most powerful of all. Focus on your relationship with money, rather than how much is under the mattress, and you will make great strides towards being its master, not its slave.

Assumption 6: Real work only gets done in real offices

Technology has enabled us to challenge old assumptions about where and how we should work. The new reality is soloists are free to conduct their business from wherever they like. The comfort of their home. Or garden. Or local café. Or anywhere!

Sociologist Dr Jem Bendell explains how the information revolution has helped reshape the modern work culture in a decidedly pro-solo way:

> While communication technologies initially have enabled large organisations to manage relations across time and space more easily, and so grow to mammoth proportions, they have also allowed the minnows of the market, including individuals, to communicate and coordinate cheaply, reducing the

need for us to be in the same place at the same time. Today, people aren't only escaping the office, but also 'the organisation', in its traditional fixed form.

Have you tried using the Internet to experiment with turning a hobby into a money-making exercise? Take inspiration from Sophie, a business analyst and online bookseller:

> I'd always been interested in first edition books. By the time I left university in the early 1990s I had quite a collection. I used to swap and sell my books through local dealers, although often it could take weeks, or even months, to sell anything or seek out books I was after.
>
> Then along came eBay and suddenly there was a mechanism for directly exhibiting my books to a worldwide market. Before long, I'd gone from selling two books a month, to two a day at one point. I started to think of trading books as less of a hobby, more of a business.
>
> Along the way I developed vital skills. For example, I noticed the language I used in the adverts would influence the price, so I soon became savvy with basic marketing principles. My negotiation skills improved as I struck deals with other first edition fanatics in order to expand my collection.
>
> In my own modest way, I'd become an entrepreneur, although I'd never thought of myself like that previously!

Assumption 7: Soloists miss out on the social elements of work

The new reality reworks the old saying 'No man is an island' by insisting 'No soloist is an island'. Sure, isolation can be an issue, but it need not be. There is a very healthy community of soloists out there and because it comprises individuals facing similar sorts of issues, you can be assured of a sense of belonging if you make the effort to participate.

There are a number of networking groups made up of fellow soloists who, like you, are keen to build new relationships, find new clients, discuss business ideas and generally enjoy the camaraderie of like-minded individuals. Seek out a networking group relevant to your industry and go along to a meeting. In the event you can't find a group to join, you could always start one, as we discuss later.

Writer and trainer Paul Jones started the Last Thursday Club so he could meet fellow creatives and discuss trends, share leads and make friends. Based in Sydney, the LTC went from a handful of people sitting round a pub table to a high-profile networking group with over 1400 members within the space of a year.

The Internet provides further opportunities for soloists to come together, not physically, perhaps, but virtually. Its ability to inform, educate and connect individuals makes the Internet a trusty companion for the lone worker. Discussion forums, newsletters and free resources targeted to soloists abound. As a starting point, you can join our online community at <www.flyingsolo.org>.

At times, all soloists need support from more experienced individuals. Happily, soloism has rekindled the apprentice/tradesman relationship, with mentoring amongst independents extremely common. Experienced soloists are generally very willing to share their wisdom with newbie mentorees, many of whom end up becoming mentors themselves. Everyone's a winner.

With so many avenues for communing open to soloists, it makes the social elements of a traditional job seem a bit hit and miss. The last word on this goes to Tim, a character from one of BBC TV's biggest comedy successes, *The Office*, who observes of colleagues, 'Probably all you've got in common is the fact that you walk around on the same bit of carpet for eight hours a day'.

Assumption 8: It is better to work hard now so you can enjoy life later

Whatever you do, don't fall for this. We all know people who postponed their happiness for a day that ended up never coming. Enjoyment simply must be a part of now. Live for the present and enjoy it to the full. The end.

THE 'C' WORD

If the stress resulting from trying to resist change could be transformed into energy, most of us wouldn't have electricity bills. The reality is change is an inevitable consequence of soloism and even the most dogmatic of us have to become flexible enough to embrace it.

We've talked a lot in this chapter about challenging and changing your point of view. What you've read so far presupposes you are capable of changing your attitude. And you are; we share leadership expert Stephen Covey's belief that 'our ultimate freedom is the right and power to decide how anybody outside ourselves will affect us'.

Robert shares an example of a time he was confronted with the need to change his thinking:

For many years, I started my day convinced I was not a morning person. Until a couple of strong coffees had worked their magic I was abrupt, grumpy and unhelpful. I acted like someone who was not a morning person and that quite simply became my operating system.

This state of affairs went unchallenged until the birth of our son four years ago necessitated a sudden change in thinking. From his arrival on planet Earth a new operating system was required.

There was just too much going on early in the day and if I was going to play any sort of useful and fulfilling role in the new world of family, I had to get up and get involved.

Four years on I'm doing fine as a morning person—why, I even present at breakfast meetings!

Still dubious of your ability to change, or worse, does the very thought of it make you queasy? If so, we've included an exercise to help.

'CHANGE YOUR THINKING' MAKEOVER

You absolutely can modify how you operate and the starting point is to change your thinking. This is an especially powerful concept for those who are seeking a greater love of their work.

The place for you to start is to seek out which trains of thought are stopping you from making progress. Look to fully understand why they are so unhelpful. Try putting any such thoughts through this four-step 'Change your thinking' makeover.

1 **Describe your current thinking in detail.** Try to focus on parts of your thinking you suspect are flawed or holding you back. A good approach is to write an imaginary letter to someone who has offered to help you or to someone whose help you would appreciate. Be thorough and be clear.

2 **Explain why it no longer works.** Continue your letter and explain why this thinking ceases to work for you. In what way does it hold you back? Again, be precise and detailed. The more work you put in to this the more chance you'll follow a new pattern.

3 **Explore a better way.** In your letter introduce a new way of thinking. Hopefully this chapter has given you some food for thought on this front. Explain why it would be so much better and really imagine yourself holding this thought. As you write, look around and consider the impact your new thinking will have on others.

4 **Actions as well as words.** Make a commitment to action. Jot down three to five things you can do to reinforce your new thinking and plan a date to begin.

Take these steps to change your thinking and you can dramatically impact the way you operate and in so doing open the door to a fresh new perspective.

Adopt the attitude of a successful soloist as described in the next chapter to find inspiration and advice based on the experience of those who are flying solo and are loving every second.

CHAPTER 2

ADOPTING THE ATTITUDE OF SUCCESS

If you think you're too small to have an impact,
try going to bed with a mosquito.

Anita Roddick

Cultivating a mindset which mirrors that of the successful soloist is a crucial step towards growing the wings you need to fly solo. This chapter we remain focused, some may say obsessed, on your mindset, but with good reason—your attitude creates a chain reaction with thoughts and actions. This fact forms the basis of one of psychology's basic principles. It is critical you appreciate the power of the self-fulfilling prophecy. Go into the land of new realities believing you'll kick ass and you will. Suspect you'll make a hash of it? Well . . .

What's more, the right attitude can:

- be a magnet for inspirational business ideas;
- open you up to possibilities you may not have otherwise entertained;
- make it easier for you to create a meaningful vision (which we talk about in the next chapter); and

- deliver small victories which serve to exponentially build your courage and confidence.

The best thing about the right attitude is that it provides a solution to the 'I don't know what on earth I'm going to do' conundrum. How? By giving you the courage to walk the walk, even when you're not ready to talk the talk. In the land of new realities, what you *can* do is nowhere near as important as what you *could* do. It may seem incredible, but once you've adopted the right belief system and developed the skills intrinsic to soloism, you will be able to 'bolt on' the vocation of your choice. Our profile of a successful soloist and the exercises that follow will help you construct that all-important template.

PROFILE OF A SUCCESSFUL SOLOIST

Through working with soloists for many years, we now recognise a pattern of characteristics that seem to attach themselves to those who make a habit of success. These individuals know how to get exactly what they want out of their professional lives. Commit to developing a handful or more of their traits to help you get out of the old assumers' groupie groove and into the soloists' zone.

Bear in mind the pages that follow contain a profile of a *successful soloist*. Thousands of soloists who embody none of these characteristics are also in operation. In fact, a number are the antithesis of the portrait—rigid not pragmatic, pessimistic not optimistic, passive not proactive. These people have as much if not more to learn from reading this than would-be soloists.

It may help to imagine that the following profile describes a character you're going to play on stage. The audience is full of your friends, family and potential clients. Can you convince them you're a successful soloist?

Successful soloists can . . . because they think they can

Firstly, and perhaps most importantly, successful soloists maintain a healthy level of self-confidence. As you read on, you'll recognise this characteristic as a common denominator amongst the others we highlight. They are particularly self-aware, naturally inquisitive and enjoy being mentally stimulated. They seek to discover what it is that makes themselves, and others, tick. They are on a constant mission to work out what their personal abilities are and how these can be put to use in the world around them. They strive for authenticity and integrity in all they do and so work to keep in touch with their values. As a result, what they do is totally congruent with who they are. Their need to express their personality through their work is paramount. Without this it's impossible for them to be happy, and successful soloists rank their happiness very highly.

Successful soloists are savvy with marketing principles

On a practical level, their ability to understand people and their motivations gives them a knack for sales and marketing, while their curiosity gives them an advantage during the question-intensive research and development stage. They show the hallmarks of a smart marketeer by maintaining a strong focus on those with whom they work. Successful soloists listen deeply to their clients and prospects and develop genuine empathy with them. Simultaneously they work out how best they can help. As a result, the product or service offered represents the best possible match between their talents and the unsatisfied needs of people in the marketplace. They turn out to be successful at selling not because they aggressively force their offering, but because they are responsive to customer needs. Finally, they don't expect to sit around waiting for the world to discover their offering—they get out there and tout their wares.

Successful soloists love their work

Because what they do is congruent with who they are, successful soloists maintain a healthy passion for their business. They love to position themselves firmly in the flow of ideas, influences and information which builds their knowledge bank. To aid their professional development they make full use of existing and emerging technologies. Gradually, they gain enough expertise to feel confident in asserting their views. Once they recognise the value of their opinions, they actively seek to share them in an array of mediums, from engaging in one-on-one conversations through to writing articles. Often, they develop great powers of observation and a sensitivity to trends which sees them regarded as experts in their field.

Successful soloists are players

Successful soloists are proactive people who enjoy participating. Their high levels of interaction enable them to become really effective at networking. They are perceptive opportunists and can often be found match-making. It's not unusual to hear them say things like, 'You're an illustrator? I met an author earlier looking for an illustrator. Let's try and find him.' This do-goodery comes back to them in spades, if not in the form of additional business, then in the form of improved personal reputation. They are masters of the virtuous circle, where their actions self-perpetuate in their favour.

Furthermore, they like to get the ear of influential people. They aren't afraid to approach them, whether for a friendly chat or to seek advice, because they are not intimidated by traditional hierarchies or status. They rarely put people on pedestals, instead having a grounded view of others and realising that however impressive influential people may seem they, along with everyone, share an essential humanity. They think the best of others, preferring to be trusting not cynical, optimistic not pessimistic. Usually their expectations are reinforced because they tend to attract and engage with people with the same open and upbeat attitude.

Successful soloists hold themselves accountable

They avoid making excuses for themselves and do not use language like 'If only I were wealthier/ better looking/ more clever', etc. They know there are enough genuine barriers to deal with without having to cope with self-created ones. Nor do they project insecurities onto colleagues. Instead of responding to others' victories with a 'Jeez, you're so lucky', they are more likely to offer a gracious 'Good on you!' Successful soloists don't regard those in the same field as competitors to be wary of; rather, they are colleagues to learn from and be inspired by.

Comedienne Rosie O'Donnell sums this up when she says, 'When I started out, some women comics were jealous of other women comics, thinking, "If she gets *The Tonight Show*, I can't." My philosophy always was, "If she did, I can too".'

Soloists who are cagey about sharing their ideas miss out on the opportunity to engage in dialogue which ultimately improves everyone's expertise. A healthier approach is to view imitation as a form a flattery. When soloist business coach Robert Middleton discovered others were passing off his ideas as their own, he dealt with it in quite an imaginative way. He found swathes of his legendary *InfoGuru Marketing Manual* plagiarised on two other business coaches websites. Rather than suing them, he considered asking them to be affiliates. 'After all, if they are so nuts about my work, I bet they could sell a marketing manual or two.' This artful use of advocates has been dubbed 'co-opetition'—an antonym to competition.

Successful soloists cherish their independence

It's amusing to observe how many successful soloists have, in the past, been less-than-brilliant employees. In their pre-solo days, many had difficulties settling down in one job and roamed from role to role like professional nomads. Their need for autonomy means other people have trouble managing and motivating them. Eventually this drive to go it alone transcends their need for a secure job.

Independence may be soloism's biggest reward, but it does come with the cost of discipline. Successful soloists have to be able to work in the absence of a formal structure and put their heads down when necessary.

Successful soloists are good with money

They also need to be disciplined with money, particularly in the early days when work flow and income tend to be sporadic. Likewise, they are willing to make financial sacrifice when necessary. In fact, many soloists master the art of being happy with less money, because for them the pursuit of it comes at the expense of the balanced lifestyle they so cherish. Successful soloists like to make up their own measures of success and often reject traditional benchmarks like material wealth and social status in favour of, say, the freedom to work their own hours or the ability to express themselves through their work.

Successful soloists have their priorities right

Emotional stability is an intrinsic part of their success and it is important to them that they are well supported by friends and family. Rather than perpetually worshipping at the altar of work, they take care to nurture key elements in their lives such as relationships and health. Many will seek opportunities for personal development such as life coaching. They refuse to allow work to dominate their lives and so are rarely resentful or fearful of it. They believe in balance, a holistic outlook and being kind to themselves.

Successful soloists keep their cool

In the face of stressful situations, they don't freak out; they try to manage the problem practically. When they make mistakes, they take responsibility for them. They are both judicious enough to recognise issues and creative enough to solve them. If they need help, they are not too proud to seek advice from trusted allies or mentors. Criticism is rarely ignored or taken to heart; rather, it is regarded as a learning opportunity. This commitment to improving requires a degree of perseverance and resilience, both qualities the successful soloist has in abundance.

Successful soloists are doers

In fact the successful soloist's overall level of commitment is crucial. They convert words into action, not just saying 'I'm going to do it' but actually taking the requisite steps. Furthermore, they make the conscious decision to make their solo career work for them from the outset rather than adopting a 'see how it goes' approach.

Successful soloists are happy to go with the flow

A new reality truth that may seem counter-intuitive to old assumers is this: provided the intention to succeed stands firm, it doesn't matter if the methodology is a little fuzzy. In fact business plans which are able to respond to the dynamics of change are a lot more useful to soloists than those which are too prescribed. Some people try to mitigate the risk of flying solo by poring over detailed plans that attempt to anticipate every possible outcome. But there is no such thing as the 'perfect plan' and those dedicated to creating one are, consciously or otherwise, employing a stalling technique. In order to progress, would-be soloists need to have the courage to face the ambiguities in their future and take the plunge in spite of them. It is vital that soloists, like their business plans, are pragmatic and are able to accommodate a degree of uncertainty. Ultimately, most agree that having the freedom to be spontaneous is one of the great joys of soloism.

Successful soloists are fearless

Finally, they appreciate the importance of facing their future head-on in order to take control of their destiny. Take this on board and you, too, can begin to guide your circumstances in a specific direction, rather than have them guide you any old where.

So how did you feel as you read this portrait? Overwhelmed or enthusiastic? Unconvinced or energised? If you feel a bit dubious, keep in mind the following:

- The profile is supposed to be illustrative, that is, no one individual necessarily encapsulates all the qualities.
- Successful soloists aren't superhuman. They still experience negative feelings like doubt and fear of failure; the difference is their ability to put these worries into context.
- Successful soloists acquire many of these characteristics as part of their journey to self-actualisation, rather than being born that way.
- Even a person with an innate predisposition to these characteristics is a successful soloist *in theory only* if they don't give flying solo a go.
- If you read through the portrait and think 'I'm just not like that', try to work out whether you could be. Pick two or three of the characteristics and try them on for size. How do they fit? If you still feel it's not you, reconsider whether soloism is a viable option.

If you're still with us, good for you! You're already demonstrating qualities we have talked about, like trust and perseverance. To help you further, we've come up with a few exercises to guide you towards 'thinking solo'. How? By asking questions whose answers will help you enhance some of the characteristics which underpin successful soloism.

EXERCISES TO ENHANCE THE KEY CHARACTERISTICS OF SUCCESSFUL SOLOISTS

Don't expect to be able to rattle off answers straightaway. You will need to apply your full powers of concentration to get the most benefit from the exercise. Try jotting each of the questions down on a clean sheet, in a pad or record them on the device of your choice. Whatever you use, carry it around with you and you'll be ready when inspiration strikes.

Self-awareness

- What qualities do you admire in yourself? And others?
- What irritates you about yourself? And others?
- Describe yourself in three adjectives. Ask three people who are close to you to describe you using the same method. Is there a discrepancy between the descriptions? Why?
- What are your favourite kinds of non-fiction books?
- If you had a free hour to be used constructively every day, how would you spend it?
- What makes you unique? Really unique? How can you make the most of this uniqueness?

- Imagine you had an opportunity to be heard by a lot of people. What would you say?

Personal development

- List five habits you'd like to change in the next twelve months. How will you change them in the next three months?
- Is there anything that, if you let go of it, would drastically improve your life or work?
- If you need help articulating your goals and ways to achieve them, to whom might you turn? A friend? A relative? A business buddy? A coach?

Professional development

- What aspects of work do you like/dislike? What can be done to improve the latter?
- What might your ideal job look like? Try to be optimistic, yet realistic.
- Are you as involved with your industry/industry of choice as you could be? Try subscribing to a relevant journal, or contributing to one you already receive.
- Research whether there are any network groups you could participate in and go along to at least two meetings.

INTEGRITY

Management guru Tom Peters reckons there is no such thing as 'a minor lapse of integrity'. This is never truer than in the case of the successful soloist.

Follow some or all of the following 'ten commandments' to help you stay true to numero uno. You can modify them to make them more personally meaningful or make up your own set of imperatives from scratch.

1 I must regularly tell/demonstrate to those people who are important to me that they are important to me. Friends, clients, contacts . . . everyone.
2 I must remain fully aware of my responsibilities as a business owner, partner, friend and parent (delete/add as applicable).
3 I must be fully present and available to those people who need my support.
4 I must show respect to all people at all times. Poor behaviour in others is not an excuse to follow suit.
5 I must make decisions when they are needed, not avoid or divert.
6 I must deliver on my promises and be true to my word.
7 I must listen more and speak less.
8 I must at all times speak up about, not step over, issues that are important to me.
9 I must acknowledge what I have, not be concerned with what's missing.
10 I must 'be my best client', treating my suppliers in the same way I expect to be treated by my clients.

Get the idea? When we're running our own ship, it's crucial to keep a handle on those things that are essential to ensure our wholeness, those things that make us complete. It may seem convoluted, but sometimes we get so immersed in 'doing it' we forget to be true to our principles. This is why it helps to have them written down.

Once you have completed work on your version, type it up (in your favourite font), print it out and put it somewhere you will see it. When the going gets tough or when procrastination and indecision are prevalent, refer to the list. Chances are something's out of whack.

By now we will have convinced you that the right attitude is standard equipment for the successful soloist. Next we need to look at altitude—how high you're intending to fly and in which direction. So pull your scarf tight and clean your goggles—we're moving on to the topic of vision. Chocks away!

CHAPTER 3
THE POWER OF VISION

'Which way should I go?' asked Alice.
'Where do you want to go?' replied the cat.
'Oh, it really doesn't matter,' answered Alice.
'Then it really doesn't make any difference which
way you go,' grinned the Cheshire Cat.

Lewis Carroll, *Alice in Wonderland*

Right, dear reader, it's time for you to start thinking seriously about your own plan. It's time to articulate, to yourself and to the world, where you are coming from and where you are going to. It's time for you to master the all-important art of visualisation. This chapter helps you on your way through an exploration of the power of vision; what it is, why you need one, how to use it to your best advantage and how to create a vision you will find inspiring and meaningful.

A vision is a mental projection of your future. It is useful because it gets you thinking about where you want your solo adventure to take you. The instant you express a vision, your goals are given substance. Visions can help you realise professional and personal ambitions—for example, 'I am going to become an award-winning architect' or 'I will become a qualified physiotherapist' (professional) and 'I will move to a house in the country' or 'I will develop a healthier lifestyle' (personal). You can even use a vision to conquer your fears.

A vision differs from a mission. The first is a picture of where you are headed; the second states a broader purpose. For example, the person whose vision is 'I will become a qualified physiotherapist' might have as their mission 'I want to contribute to the alleviation of human suffering'.

Whatever you do, don't dismiss visions as new-agey or flaky. At this point it may be hard to grasp how something so seemingly abstract can possibly be of practical use, but it truly can. For those who can't help reading about visions with a cynical eye, we'll address common doubts in the vision-blockers section later in the chapter.

Make no mistake, visions are useful for everyone, but for soloists they are indispensable. What better way to give your venture focus, energy and purpose? Your career as a soloist depends on an inspiring vision being at the heart of your venture. The best visions are based on a combination of your motivations (What do I want?), values (What do I believe?) and abilities (What do I have to offer?). Essentially, a vision enables the creation of a unique personal manifesto which can be used to guide your actions and determine your decisions.

Your vision makes sure you are where you need to be: in the driver's seat, heading in the right direction. Remarkable as it seems, visions have the power to not only guide you to your dream destination, but to act as a magnet drawing you towards it.

No wonder they are such potent weapons in the soloist's arsenal.

You may think you've never experienced the power of vision before, but we bet you have. You know when you're heading off on a much-needed holiday? On the plane, you begin to picture yourself lying on the beach. You can hear the waves breaking and smell the ocean on the balmy coastal breeze. You can feel the sun warming your skin. A smile breaks out and you start to unwind. You're nowhere near your destination, yet you've transported yourself. It's true that by using the very same method you can transport yourself into a successful solo business.

We believe the best visions are not set in stone; rather, they are living, breathing things that remain open to your questions and challenges. Later you will find advice on how to construct an organic vision that will guide you through the change and growth you will experience as a soloist.

THE BONUSES OF HAVING A VISION

The most exciting thing about a vision is that it can not only be had, but it can also be used. When yours starts working its magic, you'll wonder how you ever functioned without one. Here are just a few of the bonuses you can expect.

Decision-making becomes easier

As you move along the soloist path you will inevitably encounter forks in the road that branch off in different directions. With no vision guiding your choice, you risk picking a path arbitrarily. This will cause you to wander off all over the place, never really getting anywhere or knowing where you'll end up. With a vision, though, you have an oracle to consult whenever you need to decide which track to take. Before settling on any choice, you're able to ask, 'Does collaborating with this person/moving to this location/accepting this assignment fit with my vision?' If yes, you can proceed with confidence; if no, hit the delete button.

Management consultant Ben used the vision technique to help him on his way and today he's living his vision and loving it:

> A year before I was ready to fly solo I created my vision, the headline of which was: 'In twelve months' time, I see myself running my own business, working from a home office which has a view of the ocean.' This scenario bore no resemblance to my circumstances at the time.
>
> I knew if I really wanted the set-up I dreamed of I'd need to make big life changes over the year. It was nerve-racking in a way, but my vision helped me justify these changes. When faced with decisions, I'd refer to my vision and ask 'Does this fit?' This made my journey to soloism easier. In fact, it would have been near impossible for me to get to where I am if I hadn't had such a strong mental picture of where I wanted to be.

You stay focused

In the early days of a new business it's easy to be attracted by the bright lights of new opportunities. A vision keeps you focused on your priorities. Acting with such focus and purpose, even in the face of adversity, means you can't help but make progress. Just like the old adage says, 'the whole world steps aside for the man who knows where he is going'.

You become so productive . . .

Every time you ask the question 'Why am I doing this?', your vision provides the answer. It helps you see the method in your madness and so is a potent driving force, giving you the energy needed to clear any obstacles blocking your path. Even boring chores become imbued with a sense of purpose, making them a lot easier to execute than if your prime driver is a sense of obligation.

. . . not to mention attractive

Your enthusiasm and obvious sense of purpose has a stunning effect on your sphere of influence. If your vision truly inspires you, others will find it infectious. You'll find new opportunities coming your way as people, captivated by your clarity and vitality, want to be associated with you. If you know where you're headed and you articulate that through your work, others will be drawn to you like moths to a flame. Ponder for a moment someone whom you consider to be clear, together and focused. Like to get to know them better? Fancy working with them? Thought so.

You're never short of inspiration

A meaningful vision can be your very own portable life coach, acknowledging, challenging and supporting as you move forwards. In fact it's the best motivational tool you're likely to find.

WHAT'S OBSCURING YOUR VISION?

Let's face it, most don't have a clear and articulated vision and it's usually to do with outmoded assumptions like these:

Visions are for other people

It's a myth that visions only work for the wildly ambitious or for the world's movers and shakers. They are useful for everyone and as sure as it's the unfit person who most needs a gym membership, so it's the person without a vision who'll benefit the most from having one.

Why on earth do I need a vision?

Because if you don't have a vision you can't possibly know which way to go. A vision gives you something to stand for and, as the saying goes, 'if you don't stand for something, you'll fall for anything'.

Vision shmision—I've heard it all before

For every starry-eyed graduate employee eager to be part of their new company's vision, there's a dyed-in-the-wool cynic ready to tell them not to bother. Lack of harmony between a workplace's formal and informal culture is common and serves to erode staff's belief in the formal vision. Don't let others' shoddy treatment of visions devalue their currency for you. Besides you'll find believing in your

own vision a whole lot easier than subscribing to someone else's.

What's the point of having a vision if I can't work out how to get there?

Soloist Joanna got to where she wanted 'without worrying
too much in the beginning how I was going to get there ...
I believe that if your vision and determination are strong
enough you invent the processes you need to get to where
you want to go'.

She's right, you know. It is preferable to have a picture,
even one with large gaps, than to not have a picture at all.
At this stage, it's more important to think through the
major implications of what you are doing than get too
bogged down in detail. Rick gives us another example of
how a cluster of imprecise notions can together form a
perfectly valid vision:

> For many years, I visualised my current life—I saw my partner,
> my home and my office. I knew I lived in a sunny climate; did
> much of my work on the phone; spent my time surrounded by
> interesting and stimulating people. In my vision I knew I made
> good use of my skills and talents, but I couldn't visualise what
> I actually did! While it felt uncomfortable not having clarity
> around my vocation, I was able to hold the vision as the other
> components felt so right. The longer I held it, the more it
> strengthened my resolve. Little by little the jigsaw pieces fell
> into place. It was at a chance dinner meeting that an outsider
> finally saw what I had not seen. My jigsaw was complete. It
> turned out not to matter that the precise solution only
> presented itself some time after I began moving along the path.

It's liberating to realise that even if you have gaps in your vision, you can still make progress. Where clarity is missing, concentrate instead on substituting detail with feelings, sensations and thoughts. Imagine a game where you talk around a topic without giving away the central theme, then work on guessing the missing details. The trick is to have the courage to explore your future in spite of its ambiguities. Commit to taking a step towards it every day and the path really will rise to meet you.

Having a business plan is more important than having a vision

No, it isn't. Until now, old assumers have succeeded in forcing a sort of apartheid between work and personal parts of life. Toiling to keep the two separate has caused numerous soloists to create business plans with a sense of otherness, a plan which is expected to bring about a flourishing business in spite of the fact it shoves its owner's personal desires into the shadows. What sort of business plan is that? An utterly rubbishy one, that's what. Talk about putting the cart before the horse! But make your business plan follow a vision which inspires you and you'll achieve all your goals in record time. In fact a business plan that doesn't take a holistic approach towards what the soloist wants in their life isn't worth the paper it's written on, although you won't need to look far to find numerous examples of them. Soloists simply cannot afford to separate life from work and need to stop obsessing about finding *balance between* the two and instead focus on finding *harmony within* the two.

What I want seems so unachievable

The best visions should take you out of your comfort zone, but not into the twilight zone. While being ambitious is encouraged, being unrealistic is not. The more fantastical your dreams, the more likely your belief in them will falter; and if you don't believe in your dreams, they are as good as dead.

While daring to dream is crucial, it's equally important that any thoughts of Utopia are tempered with enough reality to make them meaningful. Aim to be a 'sensible dreamer' and cook up visions which, while challenging, are also attainable; that way you'll succeed in balancing idealism with realism. We'll look at ways to anchor your vision in reality in the 'Expressing your vision' section later in the chapter.

I can't have a vision because I don't know what I want to do

If your calling is eluding you, you need to embark on a mission of self-discovery to reveal your motivations, values and abilities, as together this trinity will point you towards your vision. Again, the exercises later in the chapter will help you get underway.

I know what I don't want in my life. Is that the same as having a vision?

No. To successfully create a vision, it's not enough to merely identify what you dislike about your current job or situation, although this is a good start. What separates the wheat from the chaff is the commitment to doing something about it. Unless you work out how you are going to deal with whatever is holding you back, you can't expect to be free to choose the future you want.

If you have been in a depressing situation that you've been complaining about for years, then it's definitely time to do something. It's up to you to either continue to look for reasons not to act (excuses) or seek out reasons to act (opportunities). Your vision of your bright new future acts as a rope you can use to pull yourself out of the mire of your own (excuse) making.

I'm not prepared to sacrifice my current circumstances

What truly underpins many of the objections we've talked about is a fear of change. The reluctance to break from the devil you know is commonly what prevents people from pursuing a new path.

To enjoy life as a soloist, you'll need to stretch and challenge your existing boundaries and limitations. You'll need to be flexible enough to embrace the unexpected and appreciate how it challenges you and forces you to grow. These sorts of changes keep our lives stimulated. It's the salt in the soup. How many times do we hear of illness or financial ruin as the precipitant of change? Such is the fate of people who avoid change. Besides, doing nothing is in itself a great risk. Donald Trump says, 'Sometimes your best investments are the ones you don't make.' As a soloist you will need to get used to facing change head-on rather than only confronting it when you're forced.

If you are still dubious, consider this: what is actually more frightening? Exploring your vision now or letting an unexplored vision haunt you on your death bed? It really is up to you.

EXPRESSING YOUR VISION

There is a Japanese proverb which says, 'Vision without action is a daydream. Action without vision is a nightmare.' So before you wander any further into Soloville, you will need a vision to guide you on your way. To get your thoughts out of your head and onto paper, we've included two vision-building exercises. The first, our Vision Sampler, will give you an understanding of the ingredients of a vision and provide you with an example of what yours could look like. It's the perfect warm-up to the second, more detailed exercise, which we've called 'Wish You Were Here'. This is where you get the chance to beef up the ideas generated in the Vision Sampler.

VISION SAMPLER

Earlier in the chapter we mentioned how worthwhile visions are based on the trinity of your motivations, values and abilities. Each of the questions below will help you unearth what is important to you, or at least get you thinking about it. Again, make notes, record your thoughts, give yourself the space to think through the issues until the answers make themselves known.

Step 1:
Come up with at least 3 answers to each question.

1 *What are you naturally gifted at and love doing?*
   This is your chance to express everything you love to do, not everything you have to do.

2 *What makes you special?*
   Jot down what comes to mind. Ask others for their view if you get stuck.

3 *What would you like to change in the world around you?*
   This will speak volumes about your values and reveal the causes you are passionate about.

4 *What do you most want to achieve in your lifetime?*
   Identify what drives you. Try listing at least three truly inspiring things. Be as all inclusive as possible; don't leave anything out because you think it's silly or unreasonable.

Step 2:
Armed with your responses to these questions, highlight one from each as the top priority.

Step 3:
Allowing for a bit of creative writing, fill out the following to create the outline of a vision. Tweak it until it flows nicely:

In my solo adventure, I'll (take the priority from question 1), using my (take the priority from question 2) to change (take the priority from question 3) and in so doing, I'll succeed in (take the priority from question 4).

Remember, this exercise will not provide you with anything like a complete vision. It's merely a sampler. Hopefully it will cause you to consider what really matters to you, plus give you an idea of what goes into a vision. Once you've completed the warm-up and your tyres are nice and squelchy, tighten the safety harness and take your place on the grid. You're ready for . . .

WISH YOU WERE HERE—MY INSPIRING VISION

It's time to enhance your vision by giving it depth and structure. Here's where we're going to probe a little further and excavate the real visionary in you.

If your vision is to be any use at all, it can't remain hypothetical. It needs to be put to use so it can begin guiding you towards your chosen location. That's why your vision needs to incorporate a time line stating how far to look ahead. We favour looking twelve months into the future. A year is quite a long way off and a lot can be achieved in that time. On the other hand, a year is not a long way off at all. We can stay very connected to events twelve months hence and remaining connected is essential when pursuing new goals.

Towards the close of the exercise you'll see a section that addresses a time three months from now and six months from now. Here you'll be asked to define actions in pursuit of your twelve month vision. Ultimately, the decision regarding how far forward to look is yours. We refer to twelve months; if this seems too close or too distant, change it.

Once you've completed 'Wish You Were Here', it will reveal the platform upon which present-day goals, strategies and actions may be planned and executed. After all, if you don't know where you are headed, how do you know in which direction to set out?

Please don't hurry through the exercise. This is your future we're talking about—important stuff! Take the approach of the sensible dreamer as you progress, to create a picture that is both achievable and believable. It will help if you read through the following pages a few times before letting your creativity run loose.

One last thing: you may like to download a Word or PDF version of this exercise and either print it out or type directly onto your own master. You would? Hop along to <www.flyingsolo.org/wywh.htm> and help yourself. Once you're relaxed and ready, turn off your phone, make a cup of something soothing and enjoy the journey.

Step 1: Words and pictures

Twelve months from now, the .... of ....
20 ..... my life will look like this:

1 *My intention is to be living in a home like this:*
   Describe where it is, what it looks like, what you see in the home. Describe how your home makes you feel. What colours surround you? What noises do you hear? What fragrances do you smell? Note: if you're already in a home you're content with, describe it devoid of those things you'd like to change or rectify, or include any elements you think are currently missing.

2 *Here's what a typical work day holds for me:*
   Describe how you are spending your time. What are you

doing? What are the characteristics of the people you interact with? How do you feel towards your work on a day-to-day basis? Weave in a picture of your office; describe it as you did your home.

3   *In my diary I see the following appointments and commitments:*
Don't forget we're looking twelve months hence. Describe forthcoming plans, current and future projects, and any pastimes and hobbies you wish to incorporate into your working week.
Note: If you rebel against diaries, substitute 'mind' in the headline.

4   *These are the most important people in my life, and this is what they are up to:*
Talk about those close to you and their relationship with you. What do you do together? How much time are you spending together? Are you communicating openly? Where possible, use language that suggests where the relationship may be headed.

5   *Here's how I am physically and mentally. This is my outlook on life:*
Describe your personal well-being. Talk about what you do to maintain your body and soul. What recreation and hobbies are you enjoying? Perhaps you're reading a certain kind of book these days, or you have chosen to learn a new skill. Perhaps you've become involved in a charity. Use this space to express what you want to be doing more of in life.

6   *Those things that really concerned me a year ago now look like this:*
    If there are points of concern not covered in your previous responses, here's the place to list them. In what ways has your current thinking evolved?

7   *The prominent images I see around my life are these:*
    List the most powerful visual imagery that has come to mind as you've completed this exercise. This may be to do with how you see yourself spending your recreation time, or what you've spent your soloist salary on.

Step 2: Actions to get you on the path

The next step is to introduce aspects of your vision into your current reality. Before you get underway on this, ensure you are totally satisfied with your responses to Step 1. If your responses fail to inspire you or if the questions did not elicit sufficient information, go back and make amendments. In extreme circumstances, totally overhaul this template and develop your own if it will create a more meaningful outcome. Use the thoughts and opinions you have generated and get them on paper while they're fresh in your mind.

Then you can move on to the following action plans:

I intend to undertake the following actions to get me on the path towards my inspiring vision:

1   *In the next three months I will:*
    List at least five actions that, if accomplished over the next twelve weeks, will signal noticeable progress along the path.

2 *In the next six months I will:*
   List at least five actions that, if accomplished over the next
   six months, will signal noticeable progress along the path.

Immediate actions

Finally, using your responses to question 7 in Step 1, reinforce
your 'Wish You Were Here' exercise by undertaking one or both
of the following within the next 48 hours:

1 *Choose a postcard* that in one image encapsulates your
   vision. On the back, write a note to yourself, from yourself in
   twelve months' time. You won't have much room, which
   will force you to distil your vision down to its most
   compelling elements. Mail your postcard and give it pride
   of place when you receive it.

2 Alternatively, *create a visual montage*, using magazine
   tear-outs or similar to select the images you find most
   compelling. If you're a techno-whiz you could computer-
   generate a picture of yourself against the backdrop of your
   ideal setting. Frame or laminate your montage or image and
   place it in a position where you'll see it often.

Step 3: Success signals

To measure how effective your vision has been in the future,
you need to come up with success signals at the outset of the
vision building process. Using these indicators you and the
world will know when your vision has become a reality. Success
signals are different for every individual. Here are examples of
questions you could ask to come up with your own:

What inward signs of success will show I've positively
moved towards my vision?

What differences in me will others notice?
How will I feel?
What will I be doing differently?

Concentrate on choosing responses which are meaningful to you, that way you ensure 'success' is defined in your very own terms.

Your answers will serve as reference points every time you want to check how well you and your vision are travelling.

Next we'll be looking at ways to close the gaps in your vision by adding some clarity and certainty to your plans. Come with us now as we step onto the soloists' stage: it's time to act solo.

ACTING SOLO

TIME TO MOVE AWAY FROM THEORY
AND POWER INTO ACTION.
WE INTRODUCE THE CONCEPTS,
YOU DETERMINE THE PACE.

CHAPTER 4
DEVELOPING YOUR GAME PLAN

*If you don't design your own life plan, chances
are you'll fall into someone else's plan. And guess
what they have planned for you? Not much.*

Jim Rohn

You've got the mindset. You've got the attitude. You've
even got the vision. Now it's time to give your solo plans
some substance. For those of you who have latched on to a
business idea, you'll find the issues, themes and concepts
we discuss in this chapter will help you turn it into a
reality. We'll cover the importance of research and
development, what a support team is and why you need
one, and explain how to surround yourself with perfect
partners.

For those of you who haven't yet got a clear idea about
how your solo venture is going to manifest itself, don't
panic. You're free to take the time you need to work this
out, but be sure you do address it. Failure to do so is what
sees nine out of ten would-be soloists ditching the idea
altogether. Don't be uninspired, though—the very fact you
are reading this book gives you a better shot at soloism
than most.

We'll spend the next few pages clarifying your answer to the million dollar question when we discuss the business of being yourself. Next we will free up your thinking by pulling you free from the uniqueness trap. If, by the end of this chapter, you are still undecided about the direction you want to take, we recommend you do some further reading in your quest for self-discovery. You'll find plenty of useful, inspirational books available. Look at the bibliography at the back of this book for some ideas or go to the self-improvement section of your local bookshop and see what catches your eye.

Once you are ready, the rest of the book will guide you through the practical, hands-on elements of running your solo venture.

For now, it's back to the business of being yourself.

TAKING ALL OF YOU TO WORK

By now you will have grasped the idea that the business of soloism is strictly personal. It's a profession where it's not only your right to be yourself, it's your duty, as soloism allows, demands, in fact, that you be 100 per cent you. As a consequence, residents of Soloville are unencumbered by the baggage of dual personality. The soloist you meet in a presentation on Monday is the same one you talk to in the pub on Thursday evening.

It's this total fit with who you are that can lead to a quite overwhelming love of work.

Shakespeare clearly grasped this concept when he said 'to business we love, we'll rise early and go to it with delight'. Spot-on, Bill. What's more, successful soloists know that being themselves (that is, being authentic) is not just good for the soul, it's very good for business. They adore their work and it adores them right back.

At the root of authenticity is a characteristic we have already waxed lyrical about: self-awareness. Smart soloists recognise the importance of *being* themselves and so put a lot of work into *knowing* themselves. Should they find inconsistencies in their character, they face up to them and attempt to iron them out. Unfortunately, plenty of soloists never bother to hold a mirror up to themselves. In a few pages we'll introduce you to a case in point, Roland, whose words and actions are at odds and whose business is suffering because of it.

Authenticity is worth striving for as it seems to act like fast-grow fertiliser on your confidence and contentment levels. Or so we found during our research, when we quizzed a small group of established and, it must be said, deliriously happy soloists. Our question to them was: How can you tell that soloism truly suits you? The one-line responses that came up indicate just how liberating authentic soloism can be:

'I no longer have to unwind. The pace of my business is the pace of my life.'
'I'm happy to bump into work contacts, even on the weekends.'
'By being myself, I seem to attract people who have similar values to my own.'
'I feel an overriding sense of freedom each and every day.'
'I thought I hated marketing and yet I can talk readily about what I do without boring the life out of people.'
'I say what I need to say and do what I need to do, without struggling with what I *ought* to say or do.'

Need more convincing? Imagine for a moment you've just won a luxury holiday and can take five people with you. Who will be on your list and why? The chances are you'll invite people you have pegged as genuine as they typically exude happy vibes that are very attractive. This is how things work in Soloville. No, people aren't always giving away holidays, but clients and other soloists regularly pull together teams and form groups and you'll be chosen because you're you, 100 per cent you.

LOVING YOUR WORK: A TALE OF TWO CAFÉS

Let's leave the touchy-feely side of being yourself for now and take a quick peek inside two cafés. This exercise illustrates how a soloist's persona impacts on the personality and success of their business. And don't think you have to own premises or be involved in retailing to fall foul of the nasties. Read on and we think you'll get the message.

Imagine two cafés. Both profess to offer good food and fine coffee. Someone who loves his work runs one; the other is headed by a miserable bugger. Here's how we think the differences are likely to manifest.

This comparison could have been extracted from the course notes of 'Why Micro Businesses Fail 101'. Unloved businesses do not retain clients or staff; they attract problems and generate negative referrals. Loved businesses attract opportunities and promote positive referrals. They evolve and prosper in a way that makes their owners happy.

	Loved café	Unloved café
Overall appearance	You can tell it's loved. Well presented, good attention to detail, feels like a relaxing environment.	Looks unloved, sloppy and dirty. Emits a 'don't-care' vibe.
Lighting, ambience, décor	Bright, happy, jovial and casual.	Dour, uninviting and uninspiring.
Cleanliness	Proud and ship-shape. Bathroom is clean, with plenty of loo paper and proper hand-washing facilities.	Dirty and neglected. Bathroom? Hold it in until you get home.
Staff appearance and attitude	Friendly, approachable, accommodating and caring.	Either hurried harried or shamefully slow service, 'customer is a nuisance' attitude.
Persona of business owner	Friendly, accommodating, genuinely interested in customer needs.	Uncaring, unfriendly, not perceptive to needs.

WHY YOU NEED TO WALK THE TALK

Acting with integrity is just as important as being authentic in Soloville. In the same way you probably wouldn't choose a time management consultant who always ran late for meetings or a tailor with poorly cut clothes, your business will not prosper if you are sending out conflicting signals. What you say and what you do must be consistent if you are to be trusted by your clients. In Chapter 5 we talk some more about integrity's role in the life of the soloist. In the meantime, here's an illustration of a soloist who appeared one way, yet behaved in another. The effect on his business has been detrimental, to say the least.

We'll protect this daft bloke's identity by referring to him as Roland. Roland is an independent business consultant who snappily tells anyone who'll listen that he 'accelerates business growth and enriches the lives of his clients'. He has some of the finest tools at his disposal in that he's very bright, presentable and capable. Yet he finds signing up new clients a continual struggle.

Roland describes his ideal client as being the owner of a medium-sized business that has been trading for a few years. While outwardly they enjoy success and prosperity, inwardly they feel bored, frustrated and lacking in motivation. Roland says, 'I am a good listener; I get on well with people and am quick to reveal the gap for my work with a potential client. Most initial meetings are high energy; they tell me it's as if a cloud has been lifted.'

In spite of Roland getting off to a good start, it is his lack of attention to fine detail beyond this first meeting that is his unravelling and is what contributes to his abysmal client conversion rate. He is, let's remember, working with people who are demotivated and frustrated. It's likely they'll be deeply suspicious of anyone offering a quick fix. He shouldn't be surprised if they seem to be looking for cracks in his armour.

Here's how he sees the situation.

> It drives me mad. I help these people get a snapshot of an exciting future only to become bogged down by petty detail. A client decided not to work with me recently simply because I'd misspelt his name and hadn't followed up on something really trivial. No wonder his business isn't going anywhere!

In his relentless pursuit of a brighter client future, Roland overlooks the client's present situation and openly resents what he sees as time-wasting on detail. He fails to show a deep understanding for the person, focusing instead on the project. The impression he gives initially is fine, but his behaviour a little way down the track is woeful.

He succeeds in talking the talk, but fails to walk the walk.

Roland proves it is not enough to talk confidently to your clients; you also need to show integrity and empathy in your actions. The clients he does have are likely to feel ill at ease dealing with him. Most of his prospects suspect he's a hustler. If only he took a moment to see things from their point of view, he would not be so quick to criticise their reaction.

As you move forwards look closely at the personality traits you currently exhibit. Do they align with the image you wish to project for your business? If not, what needs to change?

THE PERILS OF THE UNIQUENESS TRAP

While pondering what to do in their solo venture, many would-be soloists take on the approach of an inventor. They expend endless amounts of energy in their quest for the 'Eureka!' moment. Nothing disheartens them more than coming up with an idea, only to research it on the Internet and find it's already being done. Heads hung low, they go back to the drawing board and try to come up with something new.

This is what we call the 'uniqueness trap'. An alarming number of would-be soloists drive themselves into the ground because of it.

Those who are in the trap (but may not know it) think their biggest problem is coming up with an idea. In reality, it's only when you *have* come up with an unusual product or service that your problems really begin. Why? Because it can be incredibly hard to sell it. Even if it turns out to be the best invention ever, the history books tell us numerous great inventors died penniless. Today their inventions may well be part of our everyday lives, but they never enjoyed the spoils of their hard work. That's because they couldn't convince their contemporaries of the benefits of their inventions. It wasn't enough for them to merely market their offering, they had to shoulder the additional burden of trying to educate potential buyers who just didn't get what they were on about.

Most people are notorious late adopters. As recently as 1998, for example, only a third of Australian households had mobile phones, whereas today almost every individual has one. Five-plus years is a long time to wait around for people to catch on to a new offering. This illustrates that attempting to bring others up to speed can literally take years and so will do little for your immediate prosperity. Trying to educate people who are too change-averse to embrace the unfamiliar is energy-sapping, to say the least.

Your life as a soloist is made immeasurably easier if you can dispense with educating your potential buyer and crack on with the marketing side instead; in other words, tout a product or service your prospect is already familiar with. It is far, far more practical to take an existing product or service and *offer it in your own unique way*. If you want to be a dog trainer, for example, you need not be disheartened if there is another dog trainer in your area. Think of ways to make your offering different, perhaps by specialising in training dogs with specific behaviour problems. We'll explore the power of the point of difference a little later.

Once you stop trying to reinvent the wheel, you'll find your creative energies are free to flow again. Rather than sticking to the old assumption that to be a soloist you have to invent something new, why not think of ways you could improve upon an existing concept? Your best shot at success comes when you do what others do, but do it better and do it your way.

FINDING YOUR NICHE

Getting out of the uniqueness trap is all well and good, but if your solo venture is going to succeed you will need to find your particular place in the market. That's why as soon as you have decided what you are going to do, it's time to launch into some serious research and development. This is the bit where you confirm there is a gap for your product or service before you attempt to fill it.

While this is basic stuff, it can easily be overlooked when soloists are too fired up with enthusiasm, passion and outrageous optimism to look and listen to what's going on around them. But if you are to make any progress at all it is essential to get a grip on this topic of viability. So before you start hurtling down the runway to take off on your solo venture, be sure you have done sufficient work on the ground. As Tom Peters tells us, the best businesses 'test fast, fail fast, adjust fast'. Research and development (R&D) is the best way to ensure you look before you leap.

R&D is not just for the big end of town; it's essential for soloists and it need not be too difficult. In a moment we'll explore some tips, but first let's have a playful look at what R&D isn't:

- R&D is not about getting lots of support from your family and friends: 'Yeah, thanks, I know it's a great idea.'
- Nor is it having a line of credit signed off: 'Hey, the bank is behind me on this one!'
- R&D isn't your succeeding in getting some free PR: 'Wow. This thing is really flying!'
- And R&D isn't about getting swarms of people to your launch.

Alone, these are about as meaningful as a teen starlet's Hollywood wedding.

R&D is about defining your market. It first involves undertaking effective research, then taking what you've learnt and using it to improve your offering (the development bit). The aim is to tune your radar so you are sensitive to the signs of the times, your environment and market trends and needs. Whether you're in start-up mode or urgent make-over mode, designing an R&D strategy should be a key component of your game plan. We'll show you how shortly. For now, here's a story to demonstrate the way R&D puts your vision into action.

When she was on the verge of launching her business, interior designer Fiona found an interesting parallel between her approach to ocean swimming and the professional challenge before her:

Even though I lived by the beach, I had always been uncertain about my ability to swim in the ocean. While I found the water beyond the breaking waves really appealing, I was unsure how to make my way there through the waves.

One week, I decided it was time to face up to this fear and take the plunge. Before I even set foot in the water, though, for three afternoons, I watched the waves for an hour until I understood how, why and when the wave patterns were formed [1]. I also used this time to talk to ocean swimmers before and after their swim. They were happy to pass on tips about how to deal with the breakers [2]. I made mental notes in my mind as I watched how they entered and left the surf.

On the fourth day, the water was relatively calm and I knew it was time to dip my toe in. Before long I ventured out on a short swim [3]. By Friday I had enough confidence to tackle the surf. But before I went in the water, I walked out onto the rocks beyond the waves to remind myself just how beautiful the still waters really were [4].

Back on the beach I picked my moment, waiting till after a big set had come through to leap in. Soon I was swimming through the waves, moving through the water using a strong, rhythmic stroke. Before I knew it I was safely beyond the surf and immersed in balmy, turquoise waters. I'd made it!

Fiona had been procrastinating over the launch of her solo venture. But our suggestion that she take what she had learnt during her ocean swim and apply it in a business context turned out to be the inspiration she needed to take action. Below we've referred to the numbers inserted into Fiona's account to highlight how her experience can help you begin the R&D process for your solo business:

1 **Research.** Source, buy and read all the publications that cover your market to get a grip on what's going on. Similarly, attend all relevant trade shows, exhibitions and networking events. Look at what others are up to and see if and where your product or service takes things further. Target prospects you know will be interested in what you have to offer. Anticipate their questions and work out your answers accordingly.

2 **Talk to people.** Be very inquisitive and open-minded. Learn as much as you can about people's businesses. Others in your market, be they competitors, associated businesses, providers or clients, will all be able to contribute to your knowledge.

   Don't be afraid to share your intentions with others, at least in outline. Being frozen by fear that someone will pinch your great idea means you'll be doing zero R&D. Also, when you are honest about your lack of skills or knowledge, others will be eager to give advice. Act like you know it all and no one will want to help you.

3 **Explore how it feels.** If possible, start trialling what you do to selected parties. Create your space and as your confidence grows, increasingly assert yourself within it.

There's no better way of moving into the all-important 'doing it' zone than via a dry run.

4 **Keep your eye on the prize.** To get you over common hurdles like first-timer nerves or concerns about how you'll stack up professionally, keep your vision at the forefront of your mind. It will guide you to where you need to be.

Thousands of less-than-successful entrepreneurs never research or develop any of their plans. Break into their offices and you'll find filing cabinets full of acme ideas that the world will never see.

Finally, and most importantly, be very suspicious if during your R&D you discover there's nothing even vaguely like your product or service on the market. Ask yourself this question and think long and hard before answering:

> Is it really because I'm a total genius or could it possibly be because there simply is not a lucrative market?

Remember, most soloists succeed by doing what others do, but by doing it better. Finding the gap in the offerings of your competitors and aiming to fill it will give you your best chance of success.

STANDING OUT

Once you have found the space to build and grow your enterprise, you need to think about how you are going to get noticed. Some sectors of business are crowded, making it difficult to make inroads, particularly for those establishing a new business. To simultaneously run with an existing concept while standing out from the crowd takes some imagination, but it is possible. The secret is to have a point of difference.

By having a point of difference, you are in effect generating an area of specialisation. Used and developed properly, this will give you a 'unique selling proposition' (USP) which provides an answer to your potential client's question: 'Why should I give you my custom as opposed to anyone else?'

By specialising in some way, you create a reason for others to take note. By being noted, you stand a much greater chance of being remembered. This in turn leads to an increased interest from potential clients, plus it gives you a greater opportunity for word of mouth promotion and subsequent referrals.

When you become a specialist, you cannot help but speak with real clarity and purpose. You sound more focused and impressive than the poor generalist in your market, who's so busy trying to be all things to all people he ends up floundering as Jack of all trades, master of none.

To stand out, you need to be realistic. Making a big song and dance about what you see as your area of specialisation will only work if your potential clients believe what you're saying and if you're addressing an issue that is important to them. Pretty obvious, but look around you and see how many offenders you spot.

Every soloist has a USP which can be used to their advantage. Can you guess what it is? Here's a clue: look back to the start of the chapter.

That's right. The most striking USP at your disposal is you. Be sure to make the most of being exceptional.

YOUR SUPPORT TEAM

Going it alone doesn't mean having to make every decision and consider every action without the input of others. Having a support team to help you can be an essential part of your success. Often drawn from the ranks of friends and acquaintances, the members of what we might call your 'virtual board' expect little or nothing in return for their support; commonly, your prosperity and happiness is all they seek.

Being able to draw on a range of expertise will give your solo venture a real boost. Choose well and you will be energised by the synergy between you and your 'board'. Their input ensures you stay motivated and challenged because they support you as you change and grow. Even if your own skill set matches one or more of the positions we describe, having access to someone with similar talents provides valuable endorsement. As you plan your solo enterprise keep a look out for individuals who may fulfil these six special roles.

A visionary/creative thinker

We liken such people to helium balloons, bobbing about in the wind and bringing smiles to the faces of those around. A visionary/creative thinker can see opportunities for growth and development that you, being so involved in your business, cannot. To get the best out of such a person, always take a moment to set the context at the outset of a talk: tell them what's happening, what's working/what's not and give them any inklings you may have regarding possibilities for change. Then get your pen and paper ready and wait for them to start dream weaving!

An economist/realist

Boring, boring, boring. Just when you're all creatively fired up, along comes the economist/realist, with pins at the ready to burst your lovely balloon.

Truth is, we all need one of these. We don't have to do everything they suggest, but their opinion is often worthy of careful consideration. This person may well be your existing bookkeeper or accountant; if not, the ideas and suggestions generated should almost certainly be discussed with the person officially charged with counting the beans.

Having someone keep a foot on the brake helps keep you in check. Just don't allow anyone else's thoughts to dampen your vision. After all, an element of risk is standard equipment for today's soloist.

A personal well-being manager

Do you really think working long days and through the weekend is good for your health? We don't either. Just as we said in Chapter 1, you'll be no good to your business if you don't take time out to nurture your well-being.

Imagine a person whose sole task is to drag you away from your work. They take you into the open air when you need it most, help you throw away the home delivery menus you've let stack up and share stories which help take your mind off work. This is one cool person to have on your team.

If you're guilty of not looking after yourself, there will almost certainly be a well-being manager waiting in the wings. A friend or relative is probably itching to help. Appoint him or her today and enjoy the breath of fresh air they bring to your business.

A virtual assistant

An invention of the Internet age, a virtual assistant is a kind of Man/Woman Friday waiting at the end of your email for any overload work that may crop up. Regardless of how you access such a person, having someone to hand who can help out with tasks that risk taking your attention away from what you do best is extremely valuable.

We're fortunate to have a growing population of such resources, both in our cities and in rural areas. Seek and ye shall find.

A friendly geek/IT whiz

As unlikely as it may seem, there are people who actually enjoy fixing our computer equipment and who are adept at untangling clashes within our peripherals. Whatever that means.

These days we can access them over the phone, via our email (provided it's working) or through house calls. Finding your very own IT specialist can be a hugely liberating experience. It's also essential if you're to make the most of new and emerging technologies.

A guiding light

At some stage, all soloists need to enlist the support of someone who will help them see the way forward. This is where a coach or mentor comes in. As a general rule, mentors have knowledge of a specific industry and offer advice to those in the same sphere, whereas coaches are hired professionals who provide assistance which is relevant to all businesses.

Having the right coach or mentor alongside you can go a long way to providing the kind of support you need, with the added discipline of regular accountability. A coach or mentor is of most value when you have a fair idea of where you're headed but perhaps lack a degree of commitment, focus or, more fundamentally, belief.

Coaches usually offer a free trial of their services or are at least happy to meet up and discuss your needs. In order to fit in with their clients' schedules, they often have quite flexible working methods. Finding a mentor could be as simple as asking an expert in your field whether they would be willing to help you. Of course, to know who's who in your field requires you to do R&D, but you'll be doing that by now anyway. Won't you?

One final word on support teams: if any of these roles sound appealing to you, you could offer your support to one of your soloist friends.

SURROUNDING YOURSELF WITH PERFECT PARTNERS

In business as in life, keeping the right company can be one of the most important choices we make. As soloists it makes huge sense to view the people we work for not merely as clients, but as partners. A partnership is a relationship involving the input of at least two people. Good partnerships require mutual trust, reliance and commitment. While you need to make an effort for these relationships to prosper, the loyalty you exhibit is sure to be reciprocated by your clients. Provided you have chosen your 'perfect partners' wisely, of course.

Identifying who our perfect partners are (that is, who we want to work with) and actively seeking them out should be a crucial part of a soloist's game plan. All too often, though, soloists are totally indiscriminate about who they work for. They put no thought into who they want to work with and only think of their target market in terms of broad business sectors. When quizzed about their perfect partners, they typically respond with phrases like 'large corporations' or 'small businesses' or worse, 'anyone who'll pay me!' These descriptors are far too broad and will do little to assist in the development of solo businesses.

In the same way that we're more likely to find a life partner by getting clear on precisely the kind of person we're looking for, in business we're more likely to succeed if we know a great deal about who we are pursuing and why. Once you have worked out who makes your perfect partner, you can then seek out ways of attracting them to you.

When you have a clear picture of your perfect partner it sharpens your marketing style, thus saving precious time and energy. You are able to spot the attributes and optimum type of person to spend time with, so you get to wave goodbye to the frustrations of time-wasters. When you encounter people who fit your profile you quickly discover the most precise and informative answers to their questions. With the 'right' person in front of you, you are able to chat about your business benefits with ease. This, in turn, enhances your networking skills.

This is all good in theory, of course, but even those who have identified their perfect partners can find it tough to keep their focus while pursuing them. If your vision of perfect partners isn't clear enough, you may suffer the fate of many soloists who, while starting out with the best of intentions, quickly find their ideals diluted. The reason for this is usually a general weakening of intention through circumstance. It doesn't take long for our business to be dominated by far from perfect partners.

Web designer David explains how his business suffered when he got distracted from the picture of his perfect partner:

> I had a clear picture of who I wanted to work with and set about trying to promote my services to them. Without the back-up and portfolio of an established business, I soon found that business development was going to take a while. In the interim I started taking on smaller, less profitable jobs and soon found myself working crazy hours on the kind of projects I did ten years ago!
>
> Now, two years on, I feel trapped in a business that looks and feels different to the one I wanted to build. I have no time to promote to the clients I want to work with, nor do I have any relevant samples to show them. The last straw was when my one large client, who followed me after I left my employer, went back to my old employer as they were seen as better suited to handle the work. They were my dream client, my perfect partner. I was gutted. Where did I go wrong?

When David started his business he defined his target market, undertook some research and made his plans. Then he got sidetracked. He took one step away from his picture of perfection, thinking he would get back on track at some time in the future. As it turned out, his resolve wasn't sufficiently strong to stop him taking further steps away from his perfect partners and all of a sudden he had veered so far away they no longer considered him worthy of hiring.

Many small business failures come as a consequence of the business developing in the wrong direction, and that's invariably due to a lack of commitment to a particular path. If we don't stand our ground, we risk replacing ideal clients with clients from hell, life/work balance becoming imbalance, and control of destiny being replaced by servitude and slavery!

To truly master the concept of perfect partners and to have it work for you, what's needed is a written profile. We asked David to complete this exercise to illustrate his perfect partner profile.

What my perfect partners do: They are established, medium-sized enterprises, either launching their first online presence or wanting more from their existing website.

Particular favourites: I really enjoy working with innovative and energetic businesses that have a young senior management team and a workforce who clearly enjoy being a part of an exciting organisation. Ideally, businesses will be within a 25-minute journey from my home office.

Characteristics: My perfect partners are adventurous and open to new, innovative solutions. They're creative, level headed and highly professional. They have high integrity, ethics and morals and are clear and straightforward.

What they're not: They're not highly stressed, overemotional or financially disorganised. I've spent time with such individuals and find it impossible to do my best work with them.

Favourite projects: Creating a web presence that has a clear and tangible role within the business, one that gives clear benefits to customers and staff.

How they respond to me: My clients are willing participants in any activities I develop. They are interested in my work, value my support and take action when needed. My ideal clients see my role in their business as an ongoing relationship, not a one-off assignment.

How they treat me: They pay my invoices on time and do not try to haggle with my fees. They respect my working hours and rarely trouble me in the evenings or on weekends. They listen to my opinion and know they can rely on my expertise.

In hindsight, David wishes he'd undertaken this exercise from the commencement of his business. Had he done so, he would have nurtured new relationships earlier and felt stronger in his resolve when confronted by non-ideal clients and projects.

So dare we ask what your perfect partner profile looks like? Are you clear on who you want to work with, or will you set sail and see where the wind blows you? You had better be sure you know before you go shouting from the rooftops about your wares. As you are about to read, it's one thing to make a lot of noise, quite another to be truly heard.

CHAPTER 5

SPREADING THE WORD

An idea that is developed and put into action is more important than an idea that exists only as an idea.

Edward de Bono

By now we should have you thinking like a successful soloist and starting to act like one, too. You're convinced soloism is the new big thing, you've got your head around new realities, you have adopted the right attitude, have built your vision and your game plan is well and truly developed.

So you're ready to go, right? What's this . . . are you hesitating? Truth is, no matter how many hours of preparation you've put in to your solo project, it's often not that easy to start doing it. It's one thing to have clarity, quite another to move into action. In this chapter we're going to concentrate on winkling you out from under your desk and getting you into the big bright world. Even if you've been flying solo for years, this chapter will rejuvenate and refresh your approach to spreading the word.

TALKING POWERFULLY

Go to any gathering of soloists or small business owners and scattered around the edges of the meeting room you'll see a number of people clutching their drinks and avoiding the gaze of others. If cajoled to converse, their response to the question 'What do you do?' is brief and forgettable. At the other end of the spectrum, there are people who will speak to anyone, and while they have no problem talking they do have a problem being heard. Such individuals may well know their stuff inside out, but their ramblings leave people baffled. Both the simple statement, 'I'm a landscape designer', and the baffling, 'I'm an environmental special-ist concerned with horticultural planning and its impact on global sustainability', are fabulous conversation stoppers. At best, the first will elicit a response like 'Oh, that sounds interesting', which it clearly doesn't; the second is more likely to be met with stunned silence. In both scenarios, a dialogue shift towards weather and sport seems likely.

To make sure you don't waste the opportunities open to you at gatherings, you need to grasp how to talk powerfully about your work. At the heart of talking powerfully are two principles: being heard and being understood.

To be heard, you need to introduce your business so that it elicits a genuine reaction of 'Oh, how do you do that?' or 'That sounds interesting, tell me more'. You want your listener to be the one who invites you to get into the meaty side of what you do, rather than tell them all about it regardless of whether or not they want to hear it. The secret to earning their interest is to target your language and concepts for their benefit. When Fred uses the opener 'I make widgets that make café owners' coffee machines percolate at twice the speed', it has way more impact than 'I make widgets for coffee machines'. In the first statement, he's framed his offering in terms of easily understood results. Even if the person he's talking to isn't his ideal client, he or she has the knowledge they need to begin spreading a referral virus for him, and before long coffee-shop owners will be heading his way. In the second, he's talking in terms of processes, which is pretty dull and meaningless to the listener.

It is far better to be heard well by one person than forgotten by five hundred. Just ask Pauline, who shares her cringe-worthy experience in this brief incident report:

> I thought I was all ready to go. I'd done all the preparation, printed my letterheads and cards and was ready to launch my software design business to the world. At my first public airing I messed up big time. I was at an industry convention where in one of the breakout sessions I was invited to stand up and briefly describe who I was and what I did. After what seemed like hours I was asked politely to sit down. At the break, a man from the audience approached me thinking I was a web designer. I was devastated.

Pauline had an opportunity to talk powerfully about her work and blew it. Why? Because no one understood a bloody word she said! She made the all too common mistake of assuming what she wanted to say was the same as what people wanted to hear. To be understood, you need to make what you do meaningful to people who know nothing about your business. Pauline failed on this count and admits, too, to trying to impress her audience with technical lingo. Instead of impressing her audience, she alienated them.

Treat your audience as if they are obligated to decode the technical side of your business and you will lose them in moments. It is possible to get others interested in what you do behind the scenes, though, by initially couching what you do in as broadly understood terms as possible. Try this nifty technique: rehearse words that can be easily grasped by an 8-year-old. That's right, a young kid. This will preclude the use of jargon and demand that your language be clear, straightforward and interesting.

Let's look at ways Pauline can ensure that next time she talks about her business, she is both heard and understood.

Work out what others want to hear

This neat little exercise urges you to see things from your ideal client's perspective, so you can learn how to talk about your work in a way that will make them sit up and take notice.

Imagine you are in a restaurant and at the next table are a group of people who just happen to be your dream clients. You do not know them, but you quickly determine they are perfect recipients of your product or service.

What comments would you need to overhear that would elicit an 'I can help with that!' response from you? We asked Pauline, whose dream clients would be the managers of independent call centres, to undertake this assignment. Here are a couple of comments she'd love to overhear:

> 'I can't believe how frequently the details we have on-screen are at odds with what the caller is saying.'
>
> 'Yesterday I took four pages of written notes because there wasn't a section on the database to accommodate the information. I felt so silly.'

'The caller was waiting for ages while I tried to track down the answer. I mean, who designed this program?!'

Here's what we got Pauline to do next.

Develop and use a verbal profile

Having listened carefully to her ideal client's imaginary conversation, Pauline is ready to craft a verbal profile that she knows will earn their interest. A verbal profile is a succinct means of talking about what you do and who you do it for. It's no more than a few sentences in length.

Here's what it comprises:

1 A personal introduction.
2 A brief product or service overview.
3 An indication of who uses your product or service—in other words, your dream client or ideal target market.
4 The burning issues you address.
5 The outcomes of your work.
6 Things that make you different from your competitors.

With the possible exception of highly technical, specialised businesses, your verbal profile should be easily understood by complete strangers . . . and children.

Once you have started to clarify the component parts, the task is to weave these into a language and format that enables you to make a powerful verbal statement.

Let's run Pauline's business through this exercise:

My name's Pauline Ford [personal introduction]. I am a software designer [product or service overview] working closely with call centre managers [ideal target market]. I create software that gives call centre operators all the info they need right at their fingertips [burning issues]. As a result of my services, call centres not only run more efficiently but operators are much happier [outcomes].

What makes me different from my competitors is that I monitor usage and behaviour very closely and introduce improvements before being asked! [competitor differentiation]

In Pauline's verbal profile, she has addressed every one of the concerns raised by her dream client in the imaginary conversation. Now all she needs to do is get the ear of any call centre manager, or anyone who knows one, and the business will fall into her lap.

Talking powerfully need not be difficult but, like all things solo, it takes focus and preparation.

STARTING A REFERRAL VIRUS

Once we've mastered the art of talking powerfully and have some language that others both understand and are likely to retain, we are in a position to begin spreading a referral virus. Read any book on marketing and you'll be told that word-of-mouth referral is the best form of advertising. This has been proven time and time again. The astounding thing, though, is what the vast majority of soloists do to actively promote referrals. Zip. Zilch. Nada. Nothing.

This is crazy. It's time to take action to stop opportunities from falling through your fingers. Once you can talk confidently about your work there is masses that can be done to generate referrals—in effect you start your very own referral virus. Let's begin by reviewing the reasons why referrals are so totally amazing.

- When people refer others to you it's a sign you must be doing something right, which is a real vote of confidence. If for no other reason, referrals are worth seeking out because they make you feel good.
- A referral generally costs nothing as people will refer to you because they genuinely support what you do and want to see you prosper.
- A referral often converts into business because a lot of the 'selling' has been done by someone else, which means the fit between you and the potential client is good. Typically, referrals are pre-qualified, which makes the conversion rate high.
- Referral leads are warm leads, far away from the ghastly world of cold calling.
- Referrals save you time: time selling, time negotiating, time answering questions and time building a new relationship.
- The referral process means that new relationships grow quickly and have a tendency to last because trust, the key foundation to any lasting relationship, is accelerated through mutual knowledge of the third party.
- The potential audience for referrals is limitless. If one good referrer can have a huge impact on your business, imagine what effect dozens of referrers would have!

So there are plenty of reasons for loving referrals. Let's now explore how to turn the people you meet into referrers. You know the sort of person a soloist *is* should correlate with what he or she *does*, so it stands to reason your referrers need to be able to testify what you're like both personally and professionally. Let's take a look at each of these factors in more detail.

Personal knowledge

For people to feel comfortable about recommending you they need knowledge of your personal characteristics. Traits like reliability, integrity and honesty are priorities here. If anyone is going to speak up for you they'll want to be pretty damn sure you are reliable, have integrity and are honest. They will also want to trust that you can deliver what you profess to offer. People often use their 'gut feelings' to make up their minds on these factors, which makes these characteristics hard to fabricate. You can't tell people to feel this way about you—either they will or they won't—instead, let your positive actions speak for themselves and you'll soon earn people's faith. If any of these essential foundations is missing or lacking, you'll need to fix them up before you start working on a referral virus. Fail to do so and you'll be a victim of negative word of mouth, a virus that spreads about ten times faster than positive word of mouth.

It's a popular misconception that to get referrals you need to have been operating for a good while and people need to have sampled your services. Neither is true. Certainly trial and observation accelerate and intensify the extent of personal knowledge, but in the main it comes as a consequence of instinct and intuition.

Let's go back to our software designer, Pauline, for a moment:

Starting the ball rolling with referrals was much easier than I imagined. I found that once I had my spiel right and could speak clearly about what I did and who my perfect partners were, leads started coming my way and doors began to open.

What most surprised me was where these referrals came from. Often they were from people who barely knew me, but with whom I'd built a strong, almost immediate connection.

And isn't that how many new friendships and acquaintances start? The reason for the 'connection' is that your intuition tells you this person is good, this is a person who commands trust and respect.

That should be enough on personal knowledge. If you don't get it, go back to the beginning of the chapter and read everything again. It's key that you get your head around the topic before you swing into action.

Practical knowledge

Once your potential referrer is happy they know who you are, they will need to have an understanding of what you do if they are to spread the word for you. In a nutshell, all they need to know is what you do and who you do it for. Pauline's verbal profile from a few pages back encapsulates these vital elements. She could easily drop parts of this into a leisurely conversation to give a total stranger a straightforward overview of her business.

But what if she finds herself in a situation where there's no time for a leisurely conversation? What if her verbal profile seems too long-winded for the occasion? Then it's time for her to put away the big gun of her verbal profile and make a quick draw for her elevator statement.

CRAFTING AN ELEVATOR STATEMENT

An elevator statement is a short, snappy, abbreviated version of your verbal profile. It gets its name by virtue of the fact that it can be passed on in the time it takes an elevator to ride between floors.

You meet someone in the elevator on the ground floor; they leave on the first floor knowing what you do and who you do it for. They've been exposed to the virus!

Now for an elevator statement to really work it needs to be memorable, unlike the 'I'm a landscape designer' response to the 'What do you do?' question posed at the start of the chapter. Let's look at a couple more responses that are too bog-standard for our liking:

'My name's John, I'm an accountant.'

Sorry John, way too forgettable! How about:

'My name's John. I help businesses pay less tax and retain more profit.'

Mmmm, now you're talking!

'Hello, I'm Susan, I'm a massage therapist.'

Yawn. Try again, Susan.

'Hello, I'm Susan, I relax busy people and take their stresses away.'

Much better.

Get the idea? An elevator statement does not and cannot say everything. Ideally it makes an impact and elicits the reaction 'How do you do that?' or 'Tell me more!' As modern-day soloists we can use an elevator statement in a number of applications. You can use it in conversation, as part of your email signature, as a subheading on your website or on your letterheads and business cards.

Crafting an elevator statement can take time so it's important you don't rush it. Practise your words on a friend or colleague and ensure the final version sits well with you. An ill-fitting elevator statement is like an ill-fitting suit . . . you'll feel uncomfortable and look a bit silly.

WHO REFERS FOR YOU?

The next stage in the spreading of a referral virus is to understand who refers for you. Ask the question at any gathering of established soloists and you're likely to hear a surprising range of responses.

Some will say it's past customers, others that it's neighbouring businesses or suppliers. Still more will tell you it's friends, others that it's family members. And the list goes on. Just look at this lot taken from a discussion group we hosted while researching for this book:

- Business associations, sporting groups, church groups.
- Competitive businesses who are too busy to take on more work.
- Complementary businesses.

- Existing clients and customers.
- Friends and acquaintances.
- Industry bodies.
- Local businesses.
- Members of the local community.
- Members of staff.
- Neighbours.
- Networking contacts.
- Relatives, family members.
- School or university friends.
- Suppliers such as couriers, printers, ad sales reps.
- Websites.

With such diversity how can you expect to control or influence the incidence of referral? The answer, and the secret to unleashing your referral virus, is to recognise what your referrers have in common: they each believe in you and the work you do and want to see you prosper.

It really is that straightforward. Absolutely anyone who believes in you can and will refer for you. If you focus on creating and surrounding yourself with a team of such supporters you will be able to create a constant stream of referrals.

Here's how.

Categorising the people around you

The following diagram shows where people start out and where ideally we'd like them to be if they are to actively spread our referral virus by relaying our elevator statement or verbal profile on to others.

The people we're seeking to create and replicate are 'raving fans'. Raving fans actively refer for us. Another word might be champions or advocates. A raving fan really gets what you do and wants to see you succeed and prosper. The majority of established solo businesses have a handful of raving fans, and if they haven't the chances are they're the sort of operation that is overly reliant on one or two clients, and whose idea of networking is to have the odd chat with the dog under their desk.

Let's look at each of the five categories to map out how our relationships progress.

At one extreme are 'strangers'. This is the vast audience of people you have yet to meet. If you go to a new networking event, you will, in all probability, be walking into a room full of strangers. Next come what we call 'nodders': those with whom you have a nodding acquaintance. These people may know your name and have an inkling of what you do, but little more.

The third group are 'smilers'. Think of this group as business friends who raise a smile whenever you meet or speak. Smilers generally know a fair bit about you, and vice versa, and are likely to feel good about the kind of person you are and the business you run, or are about to launch. One step closer is 'huggers'. Huggers really get what you're about. Bump into one of these and you'll feel mutual warmth, you may even hug or embrace! Another word for huggers could be 'fans'. They're not raving fans, but they are teetering on the edge.

So we meet people as strangers, if we do things right they move to nodders and on to smilers. If we keep doing things right, smilers move to huggers and ultimately join our dream team of raving fans.

If as soloists we successfully surround ourselves with raving fans and maintain these key relationships, our marketing will be covered for life. Every time you nudge someone into the raving fan spot, you open the door to a potential lifetime of referrals.

Here's the deal: we're going to help you transform the people you meet from strangers into raving fans. In return, you need to give the process careful thought and get ready to connect with others.

MOVING STRANGERS TO RAVING FANS

There are numerous things you can do to draw people closer. As your solo enterprise evolves it will become clear what works and what feels right for you, which is key to creating a solo venture that will succeed. What's for certain, though, is that you will need to get out there. If you are to turn strangers into raving fans, you have to meet some strangers. There's no point hiding under your desk waiting for the world to beat a path to your door. Accept that invitation to the party. Return to that networking function for a second time. Go to that talk given by a person you've always admired. Have coffee with the soloist your friend was telling you about. In short, *get involved*.

To get you started let's look at some basic actions.

Moving strangers to nodders

Okay, so you've dusted off your business cards, polished your shoes and made it to a networking function. You're walking into a room full of people you've never met. What can you do to start some dialogue? You have to:

- resist the urge to bolt;
- bite the bullet and introduce yourself to someone;
- listen closely to what the other person is saying;
- find out about their work and life;
- be interested;
- explore common ground; and
- ask open-ended questions like 'How did you get started in your business?' This is more likely to generate conversation than 'Where's your office?'

Remember, you're not consciously selling yourself here; the purpose of this initial dialogue is to get into meaningful conversation, to give an indication of who you are and what you're about.

If you endeavour to turn a handful of people from strangers to nodders, then the next time your paths cross you can work on turning the nodders into smilers.

Let's explore how.

Moving nodders to smilers

This is where you can begin to demonstrate your consistency and professionalism in order to enhance your new contact's personal knowledge of you. Practical steps you can take include:

- staying in touch with the people you've met;
- following up on topics you've discussed previously;
- suggesting a coffee catch-up or invite your potential new friend to a function or event; and
- looking more deeply at what the other person does by asking questions and sharing an interest.

Architect Marcus had this to say of his early referral-building techniques:

My first outing as an independent operator was much easier than I imagined. Armed with my elevator statement and a heightened sense of purpose after months of planning, I attended an industry association quarterly meeting. There were probably 30 or 40 people mingling in the room when I arrived and my heart sank when I realised I knew no one. Right there and then I decided to have some fun. It was that or run away!

As I strode in I reminded myself that I was not selling. I was simply Marcus Thompson and I was here to listen, learn and make contacts. On one side of the room I saw two people standing by themselves, near to each other, but not talking. They looked very uncomfortable. I decided my mission was to make them relax and smile.

It was so easy! I simply introduced myself, at which point they introduced themselves to me and each other. Next I made some feeble joke about standing in the corners at parties.

Within five minutes we'd found some common ground —a love of flamenco dancing as it happens—and I'd shared my elevator statement. Two days after the meeting I contacted both with details of a forthcoming flamenco performance. As it turned out eight of us went along and had a great evening.

Two years on the three of us are still in contact. In the past month one of them has referred three jobs to me!

Moving smilers to huggers

In Marcus's scenario we can see those he met moved very speedily from stranger to hugger. When the connection is right, things can move quickly. Sometimes, though, it takes more time. Consider these actions to accelerate the process:

- Get into more detail about the outcomes of your work. What do people really gain as a consequence of your product or service?
- Give examples of who ideally you work with and why, and ask the same of your potential hugger.
- Expose the real you, demonstrate your integrity and honesty.

Moving from a smiler to a hugger is the stage where trust is built. Think of your own situation. How long does it take you to really get close to someone? Be patient. Be consistent. Be 100 per cent you.

Now before we get to the final step, where we move huggers to raving fans and so firmly pass on the referral virus, we must address an issue that may just be hovering in your mind. It's a criticism we heard the first time our referral virus concept was presented. From the back of a crowded room, a man jumped to his feet and exclaimed: 'But this is all so contrived!'

And he's right. The dictionary definition is as follows:

> **contrived** *adj.* deliberately created rather than arising spontaneously

For something to be 'deliberately created' you have to put your total focus towards making it happen. As you must realise by now, to succeed solo you must be focused and proactive. We can assure you that if you deliberately introduce this concept into your solo enterprise you *will* enjoy more referrals and get many, many more business growth opportunities. Far more than if you aren't contrived in your approach and simply leave the fate of your referrals in the fickle hands of Lady Luck.

Now for the final step.

Moving huggers to raving fans

Most established businesses, or at any rate those which exhibit reliability, consistency, integrity and honesty, have a high number of huggers and yet a much lower number of raving fans. In other words, a band of supporters who have personal knowledge of us and understand what we do and who we do it for, but haven't sent any business our way. Invariably, there's a really simple reason these huggers are not raving fans: because they have not been asked to be.

What an opportunity! A stack of people just waiting to refer and all we have to do is invite them. That's it? That's it! Think about it: if they don't know we're looking for referrals how are they going to spread the word? So the final step in spreading your referral virus is to speak up. Invite your huggers to become raving fans.

Try saying to them, 'I can see you really support what I do; would you consider acting as a referral source for me?' It's so powerful and so simple. These wonderful people want to help you but don't know how. So tell them.

Let's give Marcus our architect the final word on this:

Things had been going pretty well. I was getting enough work to keep me nicely busy, but I was growing tired of small, fiddly architectural jobs.

I decided it was time to fire up some new raving fans. Looking around my business I realised I had some great supporters and had met people who undoubtedly moved in the right circles. I reworked my verbal profile and crafted a new elevator statement that better reflected my ideal client and ideal project.

From there, I decided to host a party at my office. I adorned the walls with examples of larger scale work I had done and highlighted testimonials from satisfied customers.

Once the wine had been flowing for a short time, I gave a short speech to my small group of assembled huggers. In my talk I described my dream project and dream client and invited the assembled to keep an eye out for such people. To my total amazement, I had four leads on my desk within 48 hours!

Marcus was clearly surprised by the results. He told us he hadn't expected to hear from anyone so soon and had in fact planned to follow up in a fortnight with the offer of a bottle of champagne for a successful referral. His experience proves no such incentive is necessary; provided you can give those around you cause to want to see you do well, you can keep your bubbly to yourself!

To give your solo business a solid structure and to help ensure it runs smoothly, you will need to underpin what you have learnt with specific behaviours and actions. It's time we spelt them out.

CHAPTER 6

EIGHT ESSENTIALS FOR A HEALTHY SOLO BUSINESS

All companies have a culture, some companies have discipline, but few companies have a culture of discipline. When you have disciplined thoughts, you don't need bureaucracy. When you have disciplined action, you don't need excessive controls.

Jim Collins

When you're flying along in your solo venture, with the wind in your hair and ideally some cash in the bank, it's easy to overlook the essentials of ongoing success.

There's plenty said about the high failure rate of micro businesses in their first one to three years. Some quote figures as high as 80 per cent. Frankly, there's really very little to substantiate such scaremongering. Funny how often these figures are quoted by purveyors of quick-fix business help programs . . .

That said, it's undeniable that a number of soloists find the going pretty tough and yes, some chuck the towel in. To ensure the survival of your solo enterprise you need to instil some basic structures which we have dubbed the eight essentials. The sooner you have them in place the better, although even if you are already in business, it's not too late to set them up.

Here are the eight essentials that need to be considered:

1 Stay regular.
2 Know when and where to focus your energies.
3 Control your time.
4 Be consistent.
5 Hold your ground.
6 Build personal profiles.
7 Adopt the language of longevity.
8 Slow down, shut up and listen.

If your solo venture doesn't take the eight essentials into account you're effectively plonking a sexy-looking building onto a bed of sand: it'll look good for a short while before it starts to keel over. Take the eight essentials and lay them at the foundations of your business and you'll do just fine.

STAY REGULAR

No, we're not talking about making sure there's enough fibre in your diet, although that isn't a bad idea. Start-ups and established businesses alike often struggle with staying regular and consistent in their actions. Most recognise the benefits of having regular procedures in place, but for many their good intentions go out the window at the first hint of distraction.

So why is this?

For start-ups, the overzealous pursuit of new business can result in insufficient attention to what should be going on behind the scenes. For the established business, the pressures of servicing existing clients can take its toll on the maintenance of regular actions.

This inevitably results in one or more of what we refer to as business binge behaviours. For example, binge book-keeping, where bills are paid and invoices sent out in a mad frenzy. Then there's binge backlog clearing, where a soloist lets deadlines stack up to the point they are forced to pull a few all-nighters to clear the bottleneck. Then there's the classic, binge marketing, which is a plethora of ill-conceived advertising and promotional activity driven by knee-jerk reaction to circumstance.

While all three of these binge behaviours impact on the bottom line, they also make a massive contribution to how much we love our work. If you slip into binge behaviour you risk disturbing the balance and clarity that's integral to a soloist's happiness and prosperity.

Here, voice-over artist Caroline describes her painful slip into the world of bingeing:

Six months ago, business was going gangbusters. Not a day passed without more work landing on my desk.

I'd done a fair bit to market and promote my services and it was paying dividends. My dad always used to say 'make hay while the sun shines' and so I did. I made hay, but that's all I did.

Looking back, I just let so much slip. I'd made myself too busy to maintain business relationships. I had stopped networking. I let mail sit unopened in my in-tray and my tax return was overdue.

Then my world came crashing down. My largest client went into receivership owing me $8000 that I hadn't even got round to invoicing. My laptop containing my diary and entire database died and I hadn't backed up for months and my phone pretty well stopped ringing.

Did I start bingeing? You bet. I did everything in a panic and looking back that is precisely how it must have appeared to my clients. Thankfully, I've since picked up a new piece of business that will tide me over and allow me to dedicate some time to get some much needed structure in place.

I nearly failed through my own stupidity and it has scared the hell out of me.

Caroline's story is all too common. Many learn the need to get organised the hard way. The key to being regular is to get into the habit of spending small amounts of time keeping your house in order. Here is a suggested structure applied to an area that's highly susceptible to binge activity: marketing.

Daily actions

As any successful networker will tell you, the secret to effective marketing is to 'sow a seed' each and every day. We should absolutely be doing the same in our solo business. In practical terms this might translate to:

- Telling at least one person per day what you do, who you do it for and what the outcomes of your work are.
- Add the name of at least one potential client to an ongoing prospect list.
- Add one more personal detail about an existing client to your records.

- Send one letter/one email/make one telephone call to a new contact.

Most of these actions are directed at developing and building relationships with your customers, whether new, existing or prospective.

The main point is to have marketing be the focus for at least a brief period each and every day. Often the best way is to block out an hour or so every morning to undertake such actions. Starting the engine is the hard bit. Once it's fired up, it's relatively easy to keep it ticking over.

Weekly actions

Next, let's look at compiling a list of weekly marketing actions. These might include such things as:

- Following up the new contacts and relationships you've made during the week.
- Setting aside time to make a block of phone calls to new prospects.
- Asking past customers to respond to some questions regarding your level of service and their general impressions of your business.
- Researching your competitors, looking at how they position themselves so you can be clear on where your point of difference lies.

Monthly actions

If you're effectively handling your daily and weekly actions, your monthly actions can be a time for summarising and looking at more far-reaching strategies. This may involve re-evaluating your targets and plans and reviewing areas of your enterprise that contribute in differing ways to how your market sees you. For example, reviewing how you answer the phone, the message on your voicemail or your email signature. Along with your website and stationery, each projects an image of your personal brand to the outside world. Each area is an element of your overall marketing and as such is extremely important to the entire picture. Could any be improved? Could they work harder for you? Spend time every month considering these questions.

Finally, after banging on about how to start a referral virus in the previous chapter, we'd be very remiss if we didn't implore you to be in regular monthly communication with the people who really support and encourage your business: your huggers and raving fans.

Stay regular. Stay happy. Stay in business.

KNOW WHEN AND WHERE TO FOCUS YOUR ENERGIES

This is another issue that impacts both newbies and established soloists. It can be tempting for soloists to roll up their sleeves and get stuck in to running their business, without pausing to consider whether they are barking up the wrong tree due to their approach to certain tasks.

Unless you understand what stage you're at you cannot target your actions accordingly. Soloists who aren't clear on the stage may, for example, expend their energies working *in* their business at a time when they should be working *on* their business. Another error soloists make is to sweat about building revenue, when their time would be better spent growing their profile. Then there are the soloists who bend over backwards to find clients, when they'd meet with more success if instead they tried to enrol supporters.

Let's go into some more detail about these and other common errors which serve to illustrate the point that you need to know when and where to focus your energies.

Working 'in' versus 'on' your business

If you've been a soloist for a while, you may be a bit bored by the on/in stuff, but it is a very important topic so bear with us while we recap on it. Working in your business involves the practical elements of your work. If you're an actor, it's the acting; a gardener, it's the gardening . . . you get the idea. Working on your business involves strategy, planning, marketing or any action which enhances the practical side. Working in is the job of the practitioner; working on, the domain of the boss. Soloists do need to fulfil both roles, but are often so busy working in their business, the critical working on stuff gets neglected.

This entire chapter addresses classic working on your business issues. If by the time you complete it you're getting a bit hot under the collar due to the glaring gaps in your present structure, then you know you need to spend some time working on your business.

Don't waste your time trying to build on sand.

Building revenue versus growing a profile

Doing too much work for free or at a low cost may seem like a fool's game, but actually it can be an extremely smart way of enhancing your credibility. It is far better to give away your services in the pursuit of becoming better known than to be a $200-per-hour expert that no one knows. If you're at the stage of your business where you need to raise your profile, don't let revenue hang-ups get in the way of valuable exposure. Just because you do something for free doesn't mean there isn't value in it for you.

The trick is to identify ways to get in front of your ideal audience. Whether it's speaking to a roomful of prospective supporters, or writing an article in a popular publication, or giving prospects a free trial of your offering, consider ways to raise your profile and take action.

Marketing versus educating

We talked about this when explaining 'The perils of the uniqueness trap' back in Chapter 4. If you have a new or unusual product or service, you may need to spend time educating your prospects rather than marketing to them. That's because marketing won't work unless your potential buyer has a concept of what you are offering them. If you have an unusual offering, try putting a marketing slant on it so your prospects understand what's really in it for them. Your chances of getting your foot in the door improve out of sight once this is clear. Don't make the error of emphasising the unfamiliar. Potential buyers can't possibly swallow what they don't understand. To make your offering more digestible for them, frame it in easily grasped, outcome-oriented terms even if it does mean diluting your proposition. Once you have done a bit of business with a client and have earned their trust, you can gradually educate so they creep out of their comfort zone and into your zone. Remember: they will only be receptive once they are ready.

Finding clients versus enrolling supporters

Finding clients is rarely easy and going out in pursuit of them can be at best a gross misuse of time and at worst very confronting. We believe it's far better to concentrate on enrolling supporters and have them refer clients to you via a referral virus. Provided you're clear on who you want to work with and are happy to spread the word amongst your supporters, you will soon find clients who fit the bill are coming your way.

Thinking in these terms allows you to loosen up a little. Suddenly you're not selling yourself, but instead are building and growing relationships, which is a far less intimidating prospect.

Charging your worth versus proving your worth

Our $200-per-hour unknown expert is far more likely to be at the stage where he needs to prove his worth than the stage where he can set a charge apropos of nothing. Once he's succeeded in proving his worth he can feel confident about setting a charge he and his clients know he deserves.

If you're at the early stages of soloism or are established but in the course of changing direction, you would do well to look at the benefits of proving your worth. In practical terms it involves allowing people to trial or sample your services in return for constructive feedback, commentary and, ideally, testimonial. Don't perceive this as giving something for nothing as you can really benefit from what those sampling your service can give you. After all, it's a test drive for you as well as your client. When you're put through your paces in this way you have the chance to refine your new offering so when people buy it from you, they know they're getting value for money.

Besides, it's far better to be out there doing it, feeling it and learning from it than pacing up and down wondering why the shyster down the road is so damn busy.

Promoting versus researching

Promoting your wares can be extremely arduous if the marketplace isn't in the mood to buy. In this context, the moods of the marketplace work like fashion trends; they change and evolve and so must you. If people aren't buying, this signifies something is awry. It could be you don't know enough about your market or its buying habits and/or your perceived market is not your market. Either way, the stage you're at is research, not promotion.

Rather than trying to force a sale on a reluctant market, you are better off investigating what's influencing the mood of your buyers. Get up to speed on what's going on, then you can figure out how your offering stacks up in the contemporary climate. Better that than trying to flog metaphorical analogue TV sets when everyone has moved on to digital.

Funnily enough, thorough research with your perceived market can be the best promotion you'll ever do. There's little more attractive to a potential client than for you to show you are really interested in what they're up to. They will also give you clues about the nature of the pains they are suffering, some of which you may be able to ease.

CONTROL YOUR TIME

It's hard to imagine a worker more susceptible to the perils of ineffective time management than a soloist. There are masses of companies and products directed at improving time management and no doubt they all have their merits. Trouble is, we've spoken with numerous soloists who continue to struggle with time even though they've spent a fair chunk of it learning all about how to get a grip on it. So what's going on here?

The secret to managing time is to know what you're really trying to do with it. Here's an unfortunate example of what we mean—you're alone in a building when a fire breaks out. What do you do? Do you:

- Stare out of the window for a while?
- Call a friend and discuss lunch?
- Hop into your email and read a few messages?
- Pop onto the Internet and surf aimlessly?
- Shuffle paper around the desk for a bit?

Of course you don't. You get the hell out of the building. You have a very clear vision (being outside), a clear purpose (following that vision, being outside, staying unharmed), clear goals (being outside in the next 30 seconds) and some tangible actions (smashing the window so you can jump free).

If soloists were just half as driven, they would save twice the time!

For you to stand any real chance of making effective use of your time as a soloist, you need at the core a vision that draws you. Just like we said back in Chapter 3, your vision underpins everything. Without it you're blowing in the wind; some days the wind is in your favour and you'll make headway, some days you'll get nowhere and other days you'll get blown backwards.

Even if you have your vision, you may still find time is somewhat out of control and you just don't seem to be getting things done the way you'd like. Clearly something or someone is stealing your time. Let's look at some possible culprits.

Other people's priorities

Twenty-first century business is all about the open flow of communication and with it comes the increasing bombardment of other people's priorities. Too often time is taken up responding to the seemingly pressing needs of others. The ring of a phone, the boing of an email and the murmur of an SMS are all means of alerting us to something that has an implied urgency.

But whose urgency is being played out here? Certainly not yours.

As a soloist it's essential to keep *your* priorities at the top of your list. The customer may be right, but his sense of timing can be all over the place. Being accessible by those who genuinely need your support is laudable; allowing yourself to be available to all 24/7 is frankly laughable. Here are some ways to seize control back from the time thieves:

- Occasionally divert to voicemail so your phone isn't constantly distracting you. Or you could try a message answering service.

- Set retrieve schedules for your email program and designate a specific time to deal with them. That way you won't be tempted to punctuate your time with responding to emails as they arrive.
- Consider using multiple identities. Differing email addresses and mobile numbers for private and business contacts helps control the flow.
- Enlist the aid of a virtual assistant to help out with your admin.

Using blocks of time

Blocking out time to address your priorities is a wonderful habit to adopt and one that is easier to introduce than you may think. Blocks work in much the same way as meetings, the only difference being the meeting is with yourself.

Anna, a corporate trainer, is a strong advocate of using blocks of time. Here she tells us why:

Looking back to the start of my business two and a half years ago, it's a wonder I'm still here. In the early days, in a bid to impress potential clients I ran myself ragged responding to their demands.

I was such a mug. Of course I was in demand, I was doing so much for nothing! Instead of me managing my time, my clients were, and they were doing a shoddy job of it.

It all changed when my coach suggested I maintain a timesheet over a period of two weeks. What a wake-up call! I realised that while I had worked 80 hours over a 10-day period, I had only billed 20, which meant I had amassed three times that in hours that were totally unproductive.

From that moment on I restructured my week, got into the habit of assigning blocks of time to certain tasks and started saying 'no' to activities that were clearly of no value to me or my business.

To this day I maintain a timesheet and have immoveable blocks of time assigned to specific tasks. My grasp of time constantly reminds me of my true worth and helps me articulate the processes of my work to my clients.

Billable actions don't slip through the net anymore and my focus has improved immeasurably.

When Anna talks of 'immoveable blocks of time' she is describing a simple system which, when applied to essential tasks, can vastly improve the sense of control over your time. This makes it an incredibly useful tool for the soloist.

Time blocking works by allocating a chunk of time for particular pursuits. You make appointments for each pursuit in your diary and commit to the arrangements you have made with yourself. By allocating a block of time to an activity you are able to give it your full focus and concentration, so you achieve considerably more than if you deal with things spontaneously. At the same time you have total control over the diary and so are able to tailor the appointments to suit your unique way of working. Prefer talking to people on a full stomach? Schedule your phone calls in the afternoon. At your creative peak first thing? Allocate a block in the morning for report writing. It's all about recognising what works best for you.

We sneaked a peek at Anna's diary and asked her to talk us through her use of blocks:

Emails: Each morning I allow myself 30 minutes, from 7.30 to 8.00 a.m., to access my email. I reply immediately to any urgent emails even if only to acknowledge receipt and read and action other emails as necessary.

I have another 20 to 30 minute email block at 12.30 p.m. and again at the close of the day. By the time I leave the office at the end of a day my email inbox is cleared. I have got into the habit of never looking at my email between these blocks.

Exercise: I allocate 40 minutes three times a week for my morning walk. I go immediately after checking emails. I leave my mobile at home but take my iPod with me to capture any thoughts or ideas I have on the way. I also swing by the newsagents to buy the paper.

Administration: Every Friday after lunch I handle my admin. I find it's the perfect way to wrap up the week. I summarise my timesheet for the week, email invoicing instructions to my bookkeeper, pay any outstanding bills and check the balances in my bank accounts. I also handle any filing, clear my desk for the start of a new week and ensure I have a bottle of wine in the fridge so my boyfriend Andrew and I can celebrate the start of the weekend in style!

Relationship building: I don't like using the word 'marketing' to describe what I do at this time, so instead I mark it in my diary as 'relationship building'. I set aside a minimum of five hours per week to grow and develop relationships. This may mean staying in touch with contacts via phone or email, catching up over coffee with a potential client or planning a means of blowing the socks off an existing client by over-delivering so I can be sure to make our interaction memorable.

Lunch date with Andrew!: Once a week, Andrew and I meet for lunch out. I work from home and he's in the city so it's a good discipline to get us both out from behind our desks.

Networking/professional development: Rather than a weekly block, I set myself a target of four hours per fortnight to be spent networking or developing new skills. I may go to hear an expert speak on a topic of interest, or go to the library and read quietly for a couple of hours, or search the Internet to find out what's going on in my industry.

Time for ME: Once a week, I book out a WHIL afternoon (What the Heck I Like). Obviously this is a time where I can do whatever I choose. I may go shopping, I may go to the beach, or if deadlines demand, I may stay at my desk. What's important is it's my choice.

Get the hang of using blocks in a similar way and you are sure to reap the rewards of having control over your time. Be aware, though, that it's not always easy to maintain the appointments you make with yourself. Arch enemies of the blocks strategy are those activities that unnecessarily break up a nice chunk of time. Meetings with others are classic culprits. For example, let's assume you have a meeting 40 minutes away from your office at 10.00 a.m. Not wishing to be late, you decide to be on the road by 9.00 a.m. The meeting runs for 90 minutes, so by the time you're heading back to the office it's nearing midday. You're back in the office at 12.30 p.m. and your tummy tells you it's close to lunch. There's the morning gone. If you're lucky you'll have responded to a couple of emails, maybe taken one or two phone calls.

Now if the meeting was very productive you've done fine . . . but was it? Too often, as Anna did in her early days, soloists respond to what others deem to be important and necessary.

Smart soloists put themselves first. That doesn't mean disrespect for customers or clients, far from it; it simply means not allowing others to tell you what is most important for you. If you need a good block of time to really craft a proposal or develop your marketing plans, don't let it go. Change less important meetings to teleconferences or email briefings. Don't be afraid to say 'no' to Tuesday and suggest Thursday. Have the meeting over an early morning coffee or a lunchtime sandwich.

When you respect your time, others will follow suit. Chase around like a lunatic, however, and soon you'll convince yourself you've become one.

BE CONSISTENT

It's no coincidence that the world's biggest businesses insist on uniformity; whether you sip on a Starbucks espresso in Sydney or London it will taste identical, because Starbucks know putting consistency at the top of their menu is seriously good for business. For the first time in *Flying Solo*, we're going to urge you to take a leaf out of big business's book. Lots of soloists don't realise this, but it only takes one or two interactions with a client before their expectations of you become firmly set. To earn their repeat business you must show that they can rely on your service. If they are to come back to you, they need to be totally confident that the excellence you demonstrate will be consistent. Even minor inconsistencies in your processes can put people off. They may spot the cracks long before you and if you're not careful, you won't be aware of any problems until things start to unravel.

Here's what happened to society hairdresser Saskia:

When I started my private salon, I used to give customers a really thorough scalp massage as part of my shampooing process. As I got busier I stopped the massage. It never occurred to me that this was, in fact, a major appeal to my clientele and a real point of difference to my competitors. Only later did I realise it's what people spoke about.

Before long, I noticed appointments were dropping off. I was very worried. It wasn't until I plucked up courage to quiz a couple of my regulars that I found out what was going on. The next week, I got on the phone to my entire database and talked about my 'new and improved superb and sensuous shampoo process'. Luckily things got back on track immediately.

What a lesson! Today I constantly review my processes and ensure I know what my customers think of what I do.

It can be tempting to cut corners when you become busy. But as Saskia's experience shows, you could end up taking away the very thing your clients come to you for. The moment something slips, you risk undermining all the good faith you've built.

The first step towards ensuring your clients get the consistency they crave is to document your procedures. It may seem petty, but writing down your processes gives you the chance to really see how things appear from your client's point of view. Some procedures may seem minor, like the way you answer the phone, for example. Others appear major, like how and when you chase slow-paying clients. All are of equal importance when it comes to the picture you project and the confidence with which you can navigate the different aspects of your solo venture.

The time to start documenting procedures is Day 1. If you're already up to Day 603 then the time to start is Day 603. No excuses.

Getting started with procedures

It's best to start with the more complex procedures as they are the ones that are most vulnerable, then work your way down to the simple everyday tasks. Begin by starting a master list, continually adding new titles as they come up. Following her hair-raising experience, Saskia took a day off to document her procedures.

Description	How often?
Back up customer database	Last Friday of the month
Check stock levels, reorder as necessary	Every Friday morning
Enter details of customer survey forms into spread-sheet. Assess what is working, what's not	Every Tuesday afternoon
Renew domain name	Annually, in the first week in May
Check database, send card and money-off voucher to clients with a birthday that week	Every Monday morning

Description	How often?
Discard magazines that are two months out of date	Last Friday of the month
Arrange payment of suppliers	Every second Tuesday
Take delivery of fresh flowers	Every Wednesday
Change water in flowers	Every morning
Polish mirrors and wash basins	Every evening

On the face of it, it may seem these processes have little impact on Saskia's customers, but just imagine the comments if she lets just one slip:

'I got a birthday card and voucher from her last year. This year I got nothing.'

'The magazines were all dog-eared.'

'The last time I went to her salon, the mirrors were all smudged.'

'I really wanted some more hair wax, but they had sold out.'

And so on.

While some things on Saskia's list were self-explanatory, she felt others required further explanation. For these, she jotted down bullet points under each that describe the steps to take. For example, under 'Back up customer database on the last Friday of the month', she put in:

- Make a recurring appointment in my diary for the last Friday of every month.
- Sort through files on the computer, checking details are correctly entered.
- Transfer copy of the files onto back-up CD.

- Ensure the CD is accurately labelled before filing.

Inspired by how organised she felt, Saskia went on to produce a detailed list of procedures with a specific focus on customer interaction (see below).

I've never felt better organised and business is better than ever!' Saskia says of life post-procedures. She has learnt that in the cut-throat world of hairdressing, it takes more than a good haircut to ensure customer loyalty.

Appointment making	Answer telephone within three rings. Set phone to divert to voicemail after three rings. Return messages the same day.
On arrival	Greet with a smile. Offer to take coat and bag.
	Offer a choice of tea, coffee, fresh orange juice or, if after midday, glass of red or white wine. Accompany drink with luxury chocolate truffle.
	Offer them a seat. Spend five minutes consulting with client to find out what they want done. If open to suggestions, refer to magazine pictures to give the client ideas.
	Take them to basin. Spend five minutes on scalp massage! Ensure drink of their choice is

	waiting for them back at the chair.
	Proceed with styling.
On departure	Ask if they would like to make a return appointment.
	Check that details in the database are up to date.
	Ask if they have time to participate in a survey.
Follow-up	Call clients who have not returned after two months

Through monitoring her clients' feedback she has discovered what people really enjoy about going to her salon; it is the whole experience she offers, an experience that is consistently delivered thanks to thorough procedures.

Procedures also make life a lot easier when it comes to stepping away from your business. Should Saskia go on holiday she can print out a copy of her procedures for her stand-in. This makes both their lives easier. Plus a business with documented procedures is far easier to sell than one where all the know-how resides in the soloist's head.

When you write down your procedures, keep them in one place and add to them continually, refining and expanding as you move forwards. Once you have the outline you can start to add more detail as necessary. You may think a couple of your processes need changing or refining—for example, your email signature may not accurately reflect what you do or your voicemail message might be out of date. Whatever you think needs tweaking, carefully consider how any alterations are going to impact on your clients. Enlist the feedback, support and backing of your clients prior to making any major changes.

HOLD YOUR GROUND

If you've paid attention and taken steps to clarify your vision, done all the necessary research to confirm the viability of your venture and perfected your procedures, you're unlikely to be challenged by this essential behaviour. Still, holding your ground remains a common issue for soloists, particularly in the early days when it is easy to be overly dependent on the opinion of others. Ultimately, you will need the courage to make, and stand by, your own decisions. You need to hold your ground.

When you hold your ground, you avoid the trap of allowing any third party to dictate how you should run your business. Saskia shares her experience of this:

One of the questions on my new customer survey relates to value for money. Last month, of the 30 forms returned, one person gave this a rating of 'poor' and said she wouldn't return because of it. I was tempted to call and offer her a discount, until I realised how unfair this would be to my regular clients. If they caught wind of me giving out discounts, it's understandable they'd want one too, and before I know it I'd become a cut-price chop shop. So I chose to look at it from the perspective of, 'Well, I guess I'm not the salon for her'.

Of course if 29 out of 30 feedback forms said I was too expensive, it would be a different story. I do value customer feedback, but at the end of the day it's my business and I have to have the confidence in my offering to not allow the tail to wag the dog.

See how she's got the right balance between taking customer feedback on board and holding her ground?

Be aware that as a soloist you may be singled out as a soft target by those who want you to follow their system. If, during your solo venture, a client or supplier of yours suggests a change, do not do it unless it has unquestionable merit. The moment you succumb to changing something about how you work, whether it's reducing your hourly rate or altering the services you offer or procedures you follow, you signal to others that everything is negotiable.

Of course at times you may choose to offer a reduction in price as part of a promotion. If you reduce your fees to win a job, make sure you reduce what you do for those fees. If winning a contract demands a $10 reduction of your normal hourly rate, show the $10 as a 'special discount' on your invoices.

Never let your customers think you work for less and, most importantly, never let yourself think you work for less. You don't.

To have the confidence to hold your ground, it is essential you know where the ground is, so be sure to get in front and stay in front. There's no point grimly holding on to analogue when the rest of the world has embraced digital. Use your judgement wisely; respect your client's opinions but, whatever you do, don't let them take you for a ride.

BUILD PERSONAL PROFILES

While you're immersed in running your solo business, it's easy to overlook important events and milestones affecting the people with whom you work and interact. Yet to do so is to miss a crucial relationship-building opportunity. Developing and maintaining what we call 'personal profiles' can provide the foundation to lasting business relationships. Embrace this action and you will be amazed at the result.

In today's changed business environment, who you are is just as important as what you do. Personal relationships are now at the heart of not only our private but also our professional lives. Greed may have been good business in the 1980s, but today you'll flourish for being a nice person. It stands to reason, then, that you should be looking for ways of making personal connections with your business contacts.

This is where a personal profile comes in.

A personal profile is quite simply a collection of personal records concerning those people with whom you have a relationship of value, or potential value. It's what you automatically know and remember about your closest friends, but invariably don't know about your clients and contacts.

Masseur Steve divulges how he goes about building his personal profiles:

I try and evoke a relaxing environment for my clients, and while some prefer to keep quiet during their massage others are happy to chat. To help me remember information for the next time, after an appointment I will make some notes on the database, for example, Kate Smith is married to Hugh. They have a 6-year-old son called Benjamin, and so on. I'll also make a note of the sort of massage Kate prefers and at her next appointment I can ask about her family, plus I'm able to say, 'Shall we focus on your lower back area again?' I can tell she appreciates the personal attention I give her.

When you are aware of what is important in the life of clients or contacts, it does wonders for business relationships. Provided, of course, your interest is mostly genuine. People can smell insincerity a mile away, so your thoughtfulness needs to come from the heart. If you're going to find out when your client's birthday is only to send them a naff e-card, you may as well not bother. If you make the effort to write a card and send it so it arrives on time, they are likely to take your attention as a compliment, and after all, a compliment is the shortest distance between two people.

It may seem to you that it's easier for Steve to get information from his clients than it is for most soloists, but whatever your offering is, it's not that difficult to have people open up to you. Most people find being asked about themselves flattering—after all, it gives them a chance to talk about their favourite subject.

When considering your business's personal profile policy, it's worth getting clear on a couple of key factors. Firstly, who are the people in and around your business whose relationship you really value? Secondly, what steps are you prepared to take to recognise that value?

As we talked about earlier in this chapter, the notion of 'value' is interpreted differently nowadays. If an old assumer businessman is asked, 'Who amongst your clients do you value?', chances are they'd reply, 'The ones who give me money!' Fair enough, we must value those who contribute to our income, but the new reality insists we expand our measure of value beyond purely monetary terms.

The relationships that exist around our businesses have huge value. Our suppliers, our past customers, even our competitors. Within these groups are a number of raving fans. They are the people who talk about us to others, produce referrals and create opportunities.

Basically, if you are a naturally thoughtful and generous individual, you're laughing. That's because, in essence, all relationships are valuable relationships. Picture for a moment the signals it sends when you recall the name of the child of your photocopier engineer. What do you suppose that engineer carries with him or her to the next call? What impression of you? Imagine now a key client or customer. At the end of your most recent meeting, you ask if there's anything big planned for the weekend because you've remembered it's her first wedding anniversary. What does that say to your client? It shows her you have an interest in her life.

In practical terms, personal profiles are a record of as much information on each individual as you deem relevant to keep. This may include:

- Birthday.
- Wedding anniversary.
- Spouse/partner name.
- Children's names and birthdays.
- Names of pets.
- Favourite pastimes and hobbies.
- Favourite music.
- Key personal and business milestones, such as business launch date/completion of house renovations/years away their child is from graduation, etc.

The simplest computer technology makes recording this information a breeze. You can choose between fairly basic facilities within email and spreadsheet programs to special-ist Contact Management and Customer Relationship Man-agement tools. But don't allow any intimidation by the apparent complexity of some of these systems to become an excuse for inaction—there's nothing wrong with good old-fashioned card index systems. Indeed, many experienced sales and marketing people use nothing else, citing the action of writing and maintaining a card index system as a support to the essential 'human' element of this strategy. And remember, it has to be human to be meaningful.

ADOPT THE LANGUAGE OF LONGEVITY

Regardless of whether you're in the business of selling products or services, it's likely you'll prefer an ongoing relationship with your customers to a 'love 'em and leave 'em' encounter.

While brief encounters can be exciting in much the same way as a holiday romance, they're rarely terribly satisfying. That's because in most cases you need in-depth knowledge and understanding of your clients if you are to do your best work for them. Similarly, they are unlikely to send really exciting and innovative assignments your way until you have proven your trust and consistency.

Small wonder, then, that you can be left with a great sense of frustration in circumstances when your client decides, prematurely from your perspective, that you are no longer required. There's nothing worse than being ditched when there's so much more to be achieved, so much good work yet to be done.

Clients who do the leaving when you thought you were giving them the loving they need can clearly play quite a part in a declining love for your work. There's you being all caring and attentive, doing wonderful things for your client, thinking you are building a meaningful relationship—and in the meantime they are off flirting with someone new!

Sadly, when many soloists attempt to solve this problem, their efforts are cringingly clumsy.

What typically happens is the half-baked introduction of a structure that seeks to gain a customer's commitment for a longer period of time, yet without a rationale that has been well thought through. Sure, these so-called retainer strategies can work well, but they absolutely must show clear benefit for the customer and too often they do not.

Whether a retainer relationship is feasible within your business or not, your priority in the circumstances is to look closely at your practices and consider carefully what relationship signals you are portraying. You may want ongoing client relationships, but are you projecting that in everything you say and do? If you've suffered the pain from the business equivalent of a series of one-night stands, the chances are your 'language of longevity' needs a makeover.

Sticking with the romance analogies for a moment longer, imagine wooing a prospective life partner. How should you behave if you genuinely want this person to be with you forever? Your chances of success depend on whether you:

- show great interest in the person's family, their background and upbringing;

- take care to find out what they love and what they hate;
- look for common ground and cultivate it;
- are open to new learning and willing to share your own experiences and knowledge; and
- are proactive in helping this person's friends and family whenever you can.

In all instances, you will be showing your paramour you are looking to the future. What you say and how you behave implies a long-term commitment. Transfer this personal analogy to a business context and translate the actions into steps that you can readily apply. If you want customer relationships that last, try fully embracing the language and behaviour of longevity. Come across as a one-night stand and inevitably that's what you'll be.

SLOW DOWN, SHUT UP AND LISTEN

One of the side-effects of flying solo is that at times you're moving so fast and having so much fun you miss some of what's going on around you. In the same way as failing to be consistent can bite you on the bottom line, so can a lack of looking and listening.

Often it's less a case of missing what's going on around you, and more what's going on because of you. What your clients really receive as a consequence of your work can frequently be quite different to what it says on your business card. To be unaware of the real outcomes of your work is to miss a key selling point and, for that matter, a boost for your ego.

It could well be time to slow down, ask clients questions about your impact and keep quiet as you listen to what they have to say.

John, a landscape designer, did just that. Here's his story:

> A year ago if you asked me what I did I'd say I was a landscaper, end of story. These days I feel more like a relaxation guru and frankly my work is much more fulfilling as a consequence.
>
> This new awareness came about totally by accident. At the close of a large residential job one of my clients invited me to a dinner party along with two other couples, also past clients. Quite delightfully it turned into a bit of a 'John-fest' and I was amazed to learn what people actually got as a result of my landscaping.
>
> Apparently their marriages had really benefited from the time spent together relaxing and pottering in the garden. What's more, all agreed their lives were measurably less stressful thanks to the abundance of beauty, fragrance and colour in the space I had created.
>
> You could have knocked me over with a feather!

Not surprisingly, John has tweaked his marketing message as a result of this new learning and now has three very inspiring testimonials adorning his website.

To find out what influences you are having on your clients, try getting into the habit of carrying out a simple personal and professional appraisal of your work every three to six months. Ask them what they really get from your work, find out how their feelings have changed and be sure to listen carefully to their comments.

You may be surprised at the results.

Once your solo venture incorporates the eight essentials, you'll be able to view your business as a great building, sitting on strong foundations. No doubt you will want to keep it that way. What you need now is an ongoing program of building maintenance. In the final part of the book we will help you determine what parts of your building require regular attention and advise which parts of your empire you need to keep a close eye on if you are to keep on track.

STAYING SOLO

GETTING AIRBORNE IS ONE THING;
STAYING UP THERE IS ANOTHER.
LET'S EXPLORE WAYS OF KEEPING
THE FLIGHT DECK HAPPY.

CHAPTER 7

KEEPING ON TRACK

The time you enjoy wasting is not wasted time.

Bertrand Russell

Most solo ventures that crash land are forced to do so not as a result of a single spectacular disaster but as a consequence of a number of contributory factors.

If unchecked, any one of these destructive factors has the potential to force the whole shebang into the shape of a pear.

It's all to do with that thin line between love and hate. Both reside as close neighbours in life as they do in work. You can be loving your work one day, hating it the next. To stay in love with your business, you will need to stay on track. Over the following pages we'll look at some ways to look after yourself and your business, so you can stay happy. Not to mention sane.

CREATE SOME SPACE

We've already looked at using blocks of time to work on your business and have talked a great deal about ways of taking all of you to work. However, even with these strategies in place it can be hard to maintain the good, clear, creative headspace you need if your solo business is to stay close to your heart.

So how can you be sure of always finding the mental capacity necessary to maintain and hone your solo business, particularly when things get seriously busy? The answer is to fully get to grips with your brain capacity, or personal bandwidth. The challenge here is to create some extra space between your ears by sweeping away any clutter that resides there.

In a moment we're going to shift your mind from dial-up to broadband by introducing you to a brilliantly simple little tool, the mental equivalent of colonic irrigation. Firstly, though, let's explore the concept of clutter a little further.

What we mean by 'clutter'

The clutter we're talking about is particularly toxic, as it is the kind which fails to even get out of your head and onto paper. It's the junk that sits in your brain and bugs you at regular intervals. Keeping such clutter stored there is the equivalent of turning on a computer and launching every piece of software. Your computer's processor won't per-form well in these circumstances and neither will yours.

Ponder how liberated you'd feel if you removed the petty rubbish from your brain. How much extra bandwidth you would have, how much more effective you could be, how much more energy you could put to use thinking about less trivial stuff.

Here are some examples of the kind of clutter we're talking about that you may not even realise is contributing to a problem:

- You've got a box full of receipts you need to sort through.
- Your mobile phone is on the blink.
- Your desk is piled high with papers.
- You're running low on stationery.
- Your anti-virus software has expired.
- Your car needs a service.
- You're overdue for a haircut.
- You've not called your mother for weeks.
- You've not been to the movies in months.
- Every cupboard around you is full to bursting.
- You've made such little contact with friends they must think you've left the country.
- Your training shoes are fast becoming a collector's item.

Have we touched any hot spots yet? Chances are we have.

Scratch beneath the surface of a façade of procrastination and typically you will find an excess of clutter. What you need is to free up your creative mind from the shackles of this junk. What you need is to make space.

THE PERSONAL BANDWIDTH EXERCISE

This exercise is a simple and effective way to make space. It involves working out what you're putting up with in your work life and what you're tolerating in your private life. Here's what you need to do:

Devote at least 30 minutes of your full concentration to the initial task. Turn off your mobile, ignore your landline and email, and rid yourself of any other distractions.

- Get two sheets of paper. At the top of the first write 'In my work life, I am putting up with' and make a list from 1 to 10.
- On the second, write 'In my private life, I am putting up with' and again a list from 1 to 10. If either list goes beyond 10, that's fine. Let it run.
- Now you've moved the clutter out of your head and onto paper, it's time to rid them from your world for good! Get ready to take action.

Now:

Step 1: Prepare yourself and those around you
There's about to be a change and change can be painful. It's a good idea to advise those around you that you'll be behaving strangely for a while. You may start cleaning windows, tidying desks and cupboards, establishing boundaries.

Things are going to be different. Start believing it, start behaving it.

Step 2: Get visual/set goals/delegate
Write your list down in big letters for all to see and put a time and date for liberation alongside each. If your action involves others, put their names down. Make sure they know what's expected of them and by when.

Step 3: Set yourself a deadline—Liberation Day
Set a time by which you'll be liberated and start to imagine life in this new space.

Step 4: Reward yourself

As you work through your list give yourself rewards; even minor celebrations help to acknowledge and reinforce change. For example, what better way to celebrate your clear cupboards than with some brand-new storage units?

Step 5: Be realistic

This work requires constant monitoring, so look out for signs you're slipping into old habits. Remember, you can come back to this exercise whenever you need to.

REFRESH YOUR VISION

In Chapter 3 we got stuck into the 'essential power of vision' and its role as a precursor to creating meaningful plans for the future of your business.

Just as a business plan residing deep in a filing cabinet is of little use to anyone, so too is a vision that is out of date. As your business moves forwards, your vision will undoubtedly benefit from a refresh.

When photographer Damien put his vision under the microscope it helped create a little miracle:

My wife Lucinda helped me map out a vision for the first two years of my business. This initial vision served me well, getting me off to a great start. In it we got really clear on certain milestones and ensured I didn't get too carried away, as life balance is a big thing for us. Becoming a soloist was, after all, a lifestyle choice.

One year into the business I asked her to help me take another look at the vision and see if it still felt 100 per cent right. Happily most of it did. In fact I felt so good about what had been achieved we decided to make one major amendment as part of our vision rewrite. We had always imagined starting a family after five years of business, but as a consequence of the year one experience we decided to bring things forward.

Such was our confidence in the path ahead, Lucinda quit her job, worked part time with me and fell pregnant within three months. Charlotte Ann was born later that year, proving how your vision can really create miracles!

To reiterate a point we made before, for a vision to be of practical use it must be mutable and organic. As Damien discovered, the benefit of hindsight changes how you see your future. He adjusted his vision accordingly and so can you. It is terrific policy to annually scrutinise your vision to check whether it is guiding you in the right direction.

CALL IN THE (PERSONAL) AUDITORS

When it comes to looking at the bigger picture of your journey, a vision refresh is likely to be an annual exercise, although to stay truly connected with your work we suggest you also undertake a regular personal audit once every few months. In the land of the employed, people practically fall over themselves reviewing the performance of others. In Soloville this doesn't happen and while that may appear to be worthy of major rejoicing it does carry some risk.

Without a regular review of how you're travelling (as in you the person, not you the business) it can be easy to slip into bad habits and fail to reap the personal satisfaction you've set your eyes and heart on. As a successful soloist, you will be continually assessing your progress and unlike those poor souls in Jobland it's you who decides what's best and why.

Each person has a different measure of what's right and some people are never happy: more work and income than they can poke a stick at and still they grumble and complain. Others are scraping to make a living, yet whistling away and smiling all the time. How does that work? Well, it's either something they put in the tea or only one group gets the whole 'satisfaction and fulfilment' thing.

We all have a means of adjusting our own level of satisfaction, but in order to do so we first have to understand what makes us whistle and smile.

What follows is a short series of questions that can help tease out your present level of satisfaction and fulfilment and, importantly, highlight any areas that need work. Read the following statements and give yourself a 1–5 rating on how your current status aligns with what's said, where 1 means 'Fat chance' and 5 is 'Yup, that's me!'

A   My work is varied and interesting and causes me to stretch and grow ....

B   I am financially rewarded to an acceptable level as a consequence of my work ....

C   I am not underpaid, nor do I undercharge ....

D   I feel connected to the world and am in sufficient contact with like-minded individuals ....

E   My life is in balance. I spend quality time with my friends, colleagues and family ....

F When I look ahead, I see an exciting and challenging future ....

So, out of a possible total of 30, how did you do? In true trash-mag test style, here's our assessment:

25–30 Well done! You're doing well. Buy yourself some champagne.

20–24 Pretty damn good. Pay attention to your weakest areas though. Take yourself out to lunch.

15–19 Something needs to change. Time to get some plans in place. Eat in.

Below 15 As above, but with more urgency. Start giving yourself priority from this moment onwards.

Asking these questions of yourself on a quarterly basis and acting on the results really can make the difference between being the boss of a business you love, or a slave to a business you're slowly growing to hate.

AVOID DISTRACTIONS

Before explaining this further we need to make an important distinction between distractions and diversions. It is perfectly fine to take part in diversions which help to keep you on top of your game. By now you should know we are staunch advocates of the principle that you need to take breaks from work to function at your best. Without sufficient diversion you will become tired and lethargic, and susceptible to unhealthy distractions. The trick is to be prudent enough to judge the difference between healthy diversions and random distractions.

Even if you have the balance thing down pat, distractions are a constant challenge for the lone worker. As we mentioned in Chapter 2, soloists really cherish their freedom and independence. Unfortunately, this can mean they struggle with self-discipline, a trait central to a soloist's success. Distractions are the enemy of discipline. They come in all shapes and sizes and can be very destructive, as they tend to seize control over your time, your focus and ultimately your mood. As well as striking when you're at a low physical ebb, distractions can also come when you are unclear or hesitant of an action.

In Fairyland, an inspiring vision translated into action is all that's necessary to keep you focused and protected from distraction. In the real world, it's unlikely to be enough. As a happy soloist you'll want to feel good about your accomplishments at the close of each and every day, and avoiding distractions is a key to this. We recommend trying these distraction actions to give the process of avoidance a healthy nudge.

Look at why you're being distracted

As soon as you realise something or someone has stolen your attention, try getting into the habit of pausing momentarily and questioning your action. Are you embracing something minor so you can avoid facing a greater, more important challenge? When we are reluctant to undertake certain tasks for our business we can look for distractions and so give time to things we'd be better off ignoring. Most of the time, it is possible to give distraction the flick by facing up to the task at hand and getting on with tackling your real priorities.

If you are distracted because you're tired, take a short break and do something that refreshes you. You will make up for the time spent away by returning to your work with more energy. Sometimes it's better to take a break than waste your time trying to see through the fog of poor concentration.

Look way beyond the distraction

It is possible to pull yourself up by applying some good old-fashioned logic to the distraction you encounter. Ask yourself, 'If I go off on this tangent or get involved in this conversation/start pondering this issue, where is it likely to take me and is now the time to go there?'

This brand of mental ruthlessness will soon see you projecting a more focused persona that can dramatically stem the flow of distractions.

Set yourself a daily theme

This night-before, setting-the-scene exercise can help if you need to be pulled free from a pool of distraction. As you're shutting up shop, try establishing a theme for the next day. The challenge is to create a dominant feeling and hold it for the entire day.

For example, if you need to complete a document, you might adopt the theme of a successful writer. Clear your desk of anything unconnected with the writing assignment. Move your desk to the best possible position. Burn some aromatherapy oils. Set aside time to sit in the open air to read and review your work and plan rewards for the completion of the assignment.

Sending yourself different signals can often be all that's necessary to move your powers of concentration to a different level.

Finally, in the pursuit of a distraction-free existence don't forget to introduce boundaries to support your efforts:

- Divert your phone to voicemail for a period.
- Only look at your mailbox on one or two occasions.
- Avoid any negative or trivial gossip or activity.

CREATE YOUR OWN NETWORK

The old assumption states working alone translates to being cut off, but nothing could be further from the truth. We've worked to debunk this myth earlier. In Chapter 1, we began coaxing shy starters out from under their desks and into networking groups. One of the traits of our successful soloists (Chapter 2) was that they recognised the benefits of sharing ideas with others of a like mind. In Chapter 4 you discovered every smart soloist has a support team to keep them buoyant. Unsurprising, then, that we have a passionate belief that the people you surround yourself with are a critical component of enjoying your work. We are revisiting it here because we think your relationships with these people have the power to keep you on track.

Our last piece of advice on the topic is perhaps the most powerful: build your own network group. There is no better way for you to keep abreast of developments within your industry, uncover work opportunities and commune with like-minded individuals than through your own specialist network. In the introduction to the book *Unleashing the Ideavirus*, written with Malcolm Gladwell, Seth Godin gives networking the thumbs up when he says 'the future belongs to marketers who establish a foundation and process where interested people can market to each other'. Look closely at any thriving business and you'll find the person at the top is keeping very good company. What's more, he or she is bringing relevant people together at regular intervals. So why not get yourself a piece of the networking action?

Build your own specialist network and you can select your dream team. You get to surround yourself with individuals who are on a similar path and share your values and beliefs. As the owner of your network, you get to set the theme and call the meetings. Others in the group may do the same if they're suitably motivated, which means not only can you head your own network, you can also benefit from the activities of others.

When it comes to choosing who is in your network, open your ears and eyes to pick up what's going on around you. Once you understand who operates within your market, the rest is easy. Theresa, a graphic designer who produces brochures for small businesses, told us how she started planning her networking group:

> First, I took a step back to help me identify the sort of people who would help me grow my business. I knew if my network was going to work, the individuals would also need to have something to offer one another. After a bit of brainstorming with my friend David, who's a web developer (and a client, incidentally), we came up with the following list:

- Web developers.
- Software developers.
- Brochure copywriters.
- Illustrators.
- Photographers.
- Typographers.
- Other graphic designers.

Next, Theresa told us how she went about forming her network:

> Looking at the list, I realised to find members I need look no further than my current contacts. To start with, there's me and Dave. I have another friend who's a software developer, who regularly works with a copywriter. The copywriter knows an illustrator. The five of us have arranged a date and are meeting for the first time next month!

Theresa's first group may consist of only a handful of people but the nature of networking means that, provided those who go along deem it valuable, the word soon spreads to interested parties.

There are a couple of caveats, though. Network groups are easy to begin, but tend to be harder to maintain. Lots start out enthusiastically, then peter out after a couple of meetings. This is usually due to a lack of direction and focus within the group. To avoid this happening, you need to make sure yours has a well-articulated purpose that everyone understands and wants to benefit from. Also, you can foster a good return rate amongst members by ensuring actions agreed during your network's get-togethers are reliably followed up and developed.

To give direction to your network, why not devise a team name that reflects the focus you want? Examples of team names that have worked well are: The Prosperity Team, The Financial Independence Team, The Balance Team, The Leverage Team and so on.

So who in your swag of acquaintances might have a role in your network, and what will you call it? Work out who you need to get involved and start developing your network today.

HIRE A COACH

Another topic we've discussed and another that deserves more airtime here: the support of a coach or mentor can help ensure you and your business stay on track.

Like a sports coach, a professional business and/or life coach is a partner who helps accelerate your results. This is all about *you*: you're the athlete and you're the one winning the medals, while your coach cheers you on from the sidelines. Their job is to bring out the best in you. As well as providing inspiration, coaches provide practical advice by helping you clarify or fine-tune your motivations. Typically they facilitate a system of reporting, self-exploration and goal-setting to improve your focus and awareness. They concentrate on where you are today and what you are willing to do to get to where you want to be tomorrow. Together you will work out how to get there, using an approach that is custom-made for your circumstances.

Professional coaches should challenge you and ask lots of questions, so be prepared to wriggle and squirm. This process is good for you as it makes you think about your answers and prohibits you from ignoring the truth. Through this process, your coach will help you to distinguish between what you *say* you want and what you *truly* want for yourself. No matter how unclear things seem, you will always know the answers even if you didn't realise you did.

Soloists are ripe for coaching, as constantly keeping yourself directed and motivated can be tricky. Many sign up coaches for short periods of three to six months, to help them get through certain stages or to push to new levels.

Fabric designer Judy did just that and it proved to be a very worthwhile investment:

> After two and a half years in my business I knew I'd mastered the basics, but something wasn't right. My business had plateaued and I couldn't figure out what the next level was, let alone how to get to it.
>
> I signed up a coach for a weekly session over twelve weeks. Amazingly, things changed for the better the moment I made the commitment. Within a fortnight I had dramatically refreshed my way of working and opened up a stream of creativity that I'd long since forgotten I possessed.
>
> I very quickly clarified the next level and, feeling confident and purposeful, had no problem leaping up to it. I keep in touch with my coach and am going to sign up for another series of sessions later in the year.

It's interesting that Judy felt better the moment she made the commitment to getting some support. It is this brand of accountability that makes coaching so powerful for soloists. In many ways it is tailor-made for those flying solo. When your focus or clarity need a tweak, sign up for some support. When you're firmly back on track, cut the cord again.

There are a myriad coaching services available, with variations in philosophy, processes and, of course, price. Most offer a free trial of their services so you are able to try before you buy.

KEEP REVIEWING YOUR SKILLS

In the same way as creating a network or using a coach aids inspiration and focus, so too does professional development. This is the act of putting emphasis on the regular improvement of your professional skills and interests, so they are kept up to date. By so doing you're effectively facing evolution or revolution head-on, not hiding under the desk hoping it will pass. In the same way that a doctor or lawyer or judge has to maintain their position by study, course attendance or examination, so too each and every soloist should work to stay abreast of developments in their industry.

Professional development can refer to paying specific attention to your core skills, learning new design programs if you're a designer for example, or have to do with discovering more about time management, handling stress or public speaking and the like. It could be as straightforward as spending time reading books like this.

To keep on track it's important to determine what areas you need and want to develop and put aside time and funds to make it a priority. You will only flourish as a soloist if your toolbox is filled with the sharpest, best maintained tools.

PROTECT YOUR ENERGY SOURCES

Soloists who can't/won't/don't get away from their work every once in a while don't have a business, they have a job. And a pretty crappy one at that. It is essential you show your job who's boss by walking away from it once in a while. Failing to do so is by far the most common reason for soloists veering off track.

As a soloist, what do you suppose your best asset is? Your resources? Your clients? Your network?

No.

The answer is you. Without you, you have no business. It is very important you look after yourself because if you don't your solo venture will suffer and, worse, so will you. We've talked about working *in* your business. We've talked about working *on* your business. Now, ladies and gentlemen, we're going to talk about working the heck *away* from your business, before it swallows you whole.

If you find it difficult to justify taking time away from your work when you're busy, you may be labouring under the old assumption that leisure and play equates to idleness and ineffectiveness. Take inspiration from the Dalai Lama who's quoted as saying 'I have so much to do today, I need to meditate twice as long to get it done.' Just like his Holiness, you must acknowledge it really is okay to step away from your work and recharge your batteries. Recreation sharpens the saw and keeps you, the soloist and the human, in tip-top condition.

In fact, the new reality states leisure is not the opposite of work, but an essential part of a soloist's professional life. Successful soloists favour balance within work and play, rather than balance between the two. It's for this reason we urge you to blur the boundaries here. Let go of any sense of struggle of what you 'ought' to be doing and schedule, accommodate and fully embrace activities which boost your energy and well-being. Better that than to push them into an out-of-hours slot, because too often out-of-hours translates to out-of-the-picture, in other words it simply doesn't happen.

Working away from your business at regular times should be a standard practice for all soloists. Accountant Greg can testify to the benefits of taking daily time away from work:

> Every day after lunch, I go to the park and clear my head in preparation for the afternoon ahead. It's in the middle of the day, but I turn off my mobile. I don't think it's necessary to be available to my clients every minute of the day. Sometimes while I'm there I let my mind go blank, other times I cook up good business ideas. Either way I find it refreshing and relaxing and therefore it's as important to me as the time I spend at work.

Just consider the number of times you've had your best ideas while driving, relaxing with your family, on the treadmill at the gym or maybe even when you're in the shower. This is no coincidence: you're getting this clarity because you've put immediate pressures or issues slightly to one side. Clarity comes when you take a step away from your work.

To begin this strategy of getting away we recommend the first consideration be securing the block of time rather than the activity. You may need to pop back to Chapter 6 if you've forgotten how to do this.

Next compile a list of things you would like to do. (That's *like*, not *should*. Clear?) Use the time to do something, anything, which rings your bell. Keep it simple. Perhaps you could visit a nearby park or café. You may consider taking a drive in your car or going on a bus trip. Or stay at home and potter in your garden, if you have one, or plant a window box if you don't. The main thing is to get you out, get you away from your work.

If you doubt your ability to keep the appointment with yourself, why not get someone else involved? A friend, perhaps, or your support team's well-being manager or someone in your network. Making an appointment to take time out with a third party means you're more likely to stick to your commitment to step away from your desk.

If you like, take your trusty notebook and pen/tape recorder/Dictaphone/iPod with you on your break. As you prepare to leave your office, consider one priority issue that you would like to resolve or clarify. For example, if you need to find a couple of new clients, you might set yourself the challenge: 'What five things can I do to improve my chances of being noticed by my dream clients?' Write or record the challenge and off you go.

Now!

Are you still there?

Go!

CHAPTER 8

THE SOLOIST'S MANIFESTO

Throughout *Flying Solo* we have made frequent reference to what, in our humble opinion, makes for an enjoyable soloist experience. What follows is a summary of these attributes, presented as the Soloist's Manifesto.

We hope you'll refer back to this manifesto, using it as a 'loving your work' checklist of your own performance. If you'd like a fancy version to print out and stick up on your wall, you'll find one here: <www.flyingsolo.org/manifesto. htm>

WHY I HAVE CHOSEN SOLOISM

- Unlike employment, soloism allows me to feel liberated not obligated.
- In Soloville the playing fields are perfectly level.
- Work assumes its proper place alongside the rest of my life.
- I prefer working in the absence of a formal workplace structure.
- Soloism allows me to create my own measures of success.
- I have the freedom to be spontaneous.
- Soloism enables me to make the most of being myself.
- I get to keep my priorities at the top of my action list.

WHY I AM SO SUITED TO FLYING SOLO

- I maintain a healthy level of self-confidence.
- I'm self-aware and naturally inquisitive.
- I enjoy being mentally stimulated.
- I strive for authenticity and integrity in all I do.
- I'm proactive and enjoy fully participating.
- I hold myself accountable and do not make excuses.
- I am disciplined and responsible with money.

WHY IT'S SO GOOD FOR ME

- I have the freedom to fully express myself through my work.
- What I do is totally congruent with who I am.
- I feel an overriding sense of freedom each and every day.
- I face my future head-on. There's no hiding.
- I do not have to unwind. The pace of my business is the pace of my life.
- Soloism constantly stretches and challenges my boundaries and limitations.
- Soloism gives me the confidence to hold my ground.

WHAT I BELIEVE

- I know that if others can do it, I can do it.
- If this is a 'job', it's a damn fine one!
- I champion innovation and free thinking.

- Live for the present and enjoy it to the full.
- I respect the relationship between beliefs and outcomes and channel my thoughts accordingly.
- If I'm not passionate about my work, I need to do something else.
- With the right attitude I'll be a magnet for inspirational ideas.
- An inspiring vision must always be at the heart of my solo venture.
- Being myself is not just good for my soul, it's good for business.
- By loving my work I attract opportunities and promote word-of-mouth referrals.
- It's better to be heard well by one person than forgotten by five hundred.
- The secret to managing time is to first know what I'm trying to do with it.

THE WAY I WORK

- I run my solo business as I choose.
- I set my own pace.
- I engage and participate fully in all that I do.
- I don't need permission to take a break from anyone other than me.
- I don't need to follow the example of bigger businesses.
- I focus on what I have, not on what I do not have.
- I conduct my business from wherever I choose.
- I freely share my knowledge and wisdom with others.

- I listen deeply to my clients and prospects, developing genuine empathy with them.
- I have balance *within* life and work, not *between* life and work.
- I position myself firmly in the flow of ideas, influences and information.
- I like to get the ear of influential people.
- I take responsibility for my mistakes.
- While I may do what others do, I strive to do it better and do it my way.
- I acknowledge the role of research and development in the evolution of my business.
- I consider my clients and customers to be my partners.
- I attach great importance to the relationships around me.
- I work to surround myself with supporters.
- I do not binge; I'm consistent in my actions.
- I know when and where to focus my energies.
- I know the value of my work and charge accordingly.
- I have determined my rates and do not work for less.
- I do not carry junk and clutter in my work.
- I have a clear means of reviewing my performance and do so regularly.
- I protect my energy sources by taking breaks.
- I put myself first.

BIBLIOGRAPHY

This list includes all the references within individual chapters, as well as a few of our personal favourites.

Barr, Damian, *Get it Together: Surviving Your Quarterlife Crisis*, Hodder & Stoughton, London, 2004

Collins, Jim, *Good to Great*, HarperBusiness, New York, 2001

Covey, Stephen R., *The 7 Habits of Highly Effective People*, Simon & Schuster, New York, 1990

Crofts, Neil, *Authentic: How to Make a Living by Being Yourself*, Capstone Publishing, Oxford, 2003

Gallwey, W. Timothy, *The Inner Game of Tennis*, Pan Macmillan, London, 1974

Godin, Seth and Gladwell, Malcolm, *Unleashing the Ideavirus*, Hyperion Books, New York, 2001

Honoré, Carl, *In Praise of Slow: How a worldwide movement is challenging the cult of speed*, Orion, London, 2004

McConnell, Carmel and Robinson, Jonathan, *Careers Un-ltd: Another world is possible*, Pearson Education, London, 2002

Mackay, Hugh, *Right & Wrong – How to decide for yourself*, Hodder, Melbourne, 2004

Semler, Ricardo, *The Seven-Day Weekend: Changing the way work works*, Portfolio Books, New York, 2004

For more information, ideas and inspiration, go to:
<www.flyingsolo.org>